EX AMERICA

BOOKS BY GARET GARRETT:

Where the Money Grows, 1911
The Blue Wound, 1921
The Driver, 1922
The Cinder Buggy, 1923
Satan's Bushel, 1924
Ouroboros, Or the Mechanical Extension
    of Mankind, 1926
Harangue, 1927
The American Omen, 1928
Other People's Money, 1931 (pamphlet)
A Bubble that Broke the World, 1932
A Time is Born, 1944
A Wild Wheel, 1952
The People's Pottage, 1953, consisting of:
    "The Revolution Was" (1944)
    "Ex America" (1951)
    "Rise of Empire" (1952)
The American Story, 1955
Salvos Against the New Deal, 2001
Defend America First, 2003

Ex America

THE 50TH ANNIVERSARY OF
THE PEOPLE'S POTTAGE

BY GARET GARRETT

INTRODUCTION BY

BRUCE RAMSEY

CAXTON PRESS
2004

Introduction, endnotes and editing
'2004 by the Caxton Press

ISBN 0-87004-442-7

Library of Congress Cataloging-in-Publication Data

Garrett, Garet, 1878-1954.
  [People's pottage]
  Ex America : the 50th anniversary of The people's pottage / by
Garet Garrett ; introduction by Bruce Ramsey.
      p. cm.
  Includes index.
  ISBN 0-87004-442-7
  1. United States--Politics and government--1933-1953. 2. United
States--Foreign relations--1945-1953. 3. United States--Economic
policy. 4. Imperialism. 5. Garrett, Garet, 1878-1954. I. Title.

  E743.G32 2004
  973.917--dc22

                                                2004001585

Printed in the United States of America
CAXTON PRESS
170734

CONTENTS

Garet Garrett

A biographical sketch:

Garet Garrett was born in Illinois in 1878. When he was twenty-five he was star writer for the old *New York Sun*. Thirteen years later he was executive editor of the *New York Tribune*, having been in the meanwhile financial writer with the *New York Times*, the *Evening Post* and *Wall Street Journal*, and editor of the *New York Times Annalist*.

At thirty-eight he retired from newspaper work to devote himself to free-lance writing. Between 1920 and 1932 he published eight books and a number of widely circulated articles on financial and economic matters.

With the advent of the New Deal he vigorously attacked its neo-Marxian premises and its economic fallacies in a series of articles that appeared in the *Saturday Evening Post*. His writings there created much bitter controversy and caused the New Deal to threaten the life of that magazine. In 1940 he became editorial-writer-in-chief of the *Saturday Evening Post*, after the death of its famous editor, George Horace Lorimer.

In 1944 he wrote the notable political monograph entitled The *Revolution Was*, which went through many editions. This was followed in 1951 by *Ex America* and in 1952 by *Rise of Empire*. These three essays, taken serially, give a dramatic account of what happened in this country during the two decades following F.D.R.'s New Deal—to the spirit, to the mind, and to the social environment of a people who after a century and a half of being wonderfully free began to ask, "What is freedom?"

Mr. Garrett has recently retired to a cave on a river bank at Tuckahoe, New Jersey, where he lives very quietly with his wife, still making notes and comments on the passing show of monstrous human folly. He has just finished a book entitled *The Wild Wheel*, the theme of which is the death of Henry Ford's world of laissez-faire.

> *Mr. Garrett died in 1954.*
> *The above page of biographical notes appeared on the jacket of the first edition of* The People's Pottage *in 1953.*

INTRODUCTION
2004

By Bruce Ramsey

Joseph Sobran discovered these Garet Garrett essays "one night, long ago, at the office of *National Review*, where I then worked." As the flagship of modern conservatism, *National Review* supported the Cold War and the hot war then raging in Vietnam.

"Two questions occurred to me," Sobran writes. "One: 'Why haven't I heard of this man before?' Two: 'If he's right, what am I doing here?'"

I discovered these essays at 16 in a Seattle bookstore that specialized in right-wing opinions. The bright blue paperback was called *The People's Pottage*. The book was one of the twelve "candles" of the mysterious John Birch Society, though the author had died before the society was founded. In his day he had been a member of the mainstream press.

Who was Garet Garrett? He was a stylist, right from the first paragraph. His writing had an unusual clarity of belief, and the ominous tone of a man convinced that his country had been steered down the wrong road.

Garrett's beliefs were once the stuff of conservatism, and in 1954 his obituary in the *New York Times* labeled him a conservative. But the positions he defended—a pre-New Deal constitutionalism, an America-first foreign policy, a gold-backed currency and economic laissez-faire—are far forward of the trenches defended today by mainstream conservatism. His belief in laissez-faire would be called libertarian today. On tariffs and immigration he anticipates the nationalist conservatism of Patrick Buchanan. On foreign policy he occupies the ground that Buchanan and most libertarians share in opposition to today's Republican order.

In 1967 Garrett was new to me. Strangest was his essay, "Rise of Empire," in which he argued that in undertaking to defend freedom everywhere, America had given up the Republic. The terms of this argument were conservative, but was the conclusion? My idea of a conservative was Sen. Barry Goldwater, whose policy on overseas communism was the opposite of Garrett's.

Who was Garet Garrett? How did he pronounce his name? The book I bought in 1967 said he had retired to a cave on a river bank. A troglodyte indeed.

Thirty-five years later I went looking. I found a small academic biography, Carl Ryant's *Profit's Prophet* (1989), and a chapter in Justin Raimondo's *Reclaiming the American Right* (1990). I found 13 Garrett books, including several of what might be called economics novels (*The Driver, The Cinder Buggy*), a novelistic essay (*The Blue Wound*), a political novel (*Harangue*) and an economic biography (*The Wild Wheel*). There were acres of journalism, much of it in the *Saturday Evening Post* and a forgotten magazine called *American Affairs*.

Scattered here and there were statements about the man himself. Garrett was five feet five and had blue-gray eyes. In 1937 his editors at the *Saturday Evening Post* said he had "an apparently inexhaustible supply of nervous energy and the most completely controlled and incisively logical mind we've ever come across."

He was the son of a tinker, born in downstate Illinois in 1878 as Edward Peter Garrett. He grew up on a farm in Iowa and learned to direct a team of horses at age ten. Schooled only through the third grade, he educated himself by reading books.

He left home at 18, hopping a freight for Chicago. "It was a hard, unfriendly city," he wrote. "If you were hungry, you would let it go for a long time without asking for anything, for if you asked, you were a bum." It was there, he recounted in the *Saturday Evening Post*, that he hung his only shirt up to dry on a bush and the wind blew it into the river while he dreamed. Shirtless, he hopped a freight for Cleveland.

Garrett began his career as a printer's assistant at the *Cleveland Press*. He soon became a reporter. During the McKinley administration he moved to Washington, D.C., where he began writing under the name Garet. The name stuck, and he legally adopted it. He pronounced it GARE-et GARE-et.

In 1900, when J.P. Morgan was putting together the United States Steel Corporation, Garrett moved to New York and became a business reporter. In *The Cinder Buggy* (1923), he describes the steelmen holding court with the press. He was there. During the early years of the century he wrote pieces for investors under the pen name of John Parr. He also made a lifelong friend of Bernard Baruch, who would become a confidant of Woodrow Wilson and Franklin Roosevelt.

By 1915, when neutral America was on the sidelines of World War I, Garrett was dispensing opinions from the editorial board of the *New York Times*. The paper's owner, Adolph Ochs, wanted the *Times* to be neutral on the war. But Garrett wrote in his journal a month after the *Lusitania* went down, "Over and over I protest that we are more pro-English than the English." On February 29, 1916, he wrote: "Neutrality is so rate that I sometimes ask myself if it is not an affectation. Yet I believe in it." He would later proclaim World War I "a total loss."

In December 1915, the *Times* sent Garrett to Germany. He wrote a 10-part series and brought home an official message that Germany was willing to negotiate for peace. He met with Secretary of State Robert Lansing, who was pro-British and not interested.

In 1916 Garrett went to the *Tribune*. "I was impatient to do things, and it was hard to get anything done at the *Times*—anything new," he wrote. After the war he left newspapers, shifting his efforts to magazines and books. In 1922 he settled in at the *Saturday Evening Post*, which ran his articles and serialized his books for the next 20 years.

Garrett's early journalism was not politically flavored. As a young man, he recalled, "I took the form of government as a fact to begin with, like the fact of one's parentage, and did not think about it at all." After about 1920 his work took on a point of view.

Garrett believed in liberty and self-reliance, and not as two separate things. He was not eager to justify his belief. Some things just are, and liberty and self-reliance was who Americans were. Dependence on the state was an Old World idea, like the divine right of kings.

Liberty, he believed, makes the individual strong. In *Satan's Bushel* (1924), he pictured an old man urging farmers to be strong like a tree. The elms, the old man says, "have no sick religion of equality. They contend with each other for advantage. What they have in common is an instinct—one way of fighting against all the other plants. That is what the farmer needs."

Garrett also argued that liberty makes the nation strong. In *The Cinder Buggy*, he wrote of the first entrepreneurs of steel: "they were free egoists, seeking profit, power, personal success, everyone attending to his own greatness. Never before in the world had the practice of individualism been so reckless, so purely dynamic, so heedless of the Devil's harvest." Yet to prepare the nation for World War I, he wrote, "it happened—it precisely happened—that they forged the right weapons."

There was also an egalitarian aspect. The America he remembered (and it was probably the rural America) was a place that combined self-reliance and a kind of social equality. "To be poor is no disgrace," Garrett wrote in 1947. "In the whole civilized world that was only true here."

Keeping the American identity justified a certain separatism. Though at home Garrett was for laissez-faire, at the border he became a nationalist. In 1920 he supported the Jones Act, the law that reserved shipping between two U.S. ports to U.S. crews and ships. He didn't want America to be at the mercy of the British merchant marine. In 1924 he supported the law curtailing immigration. Immigrants, he argued, did not think like Americans.

"The new immigration is in a notable degree wage-conscious," he wrote. "Its point of view is proletarian. Previously there had been no proletariat in this country. The word was not current in the language until after the tide of migrating humanity began to rise from the south and east of Europe. There is still in the United States no proletariat but this."

In 1930 the *Post* sent Garrett to the Philippines, then a U.S. colony, where he found "sentimental imperialists" trying to mold the Filipinos into Americans. Garrett, who made no effort to hide his belief in American ways, concluded that socially engineering the Filipino culture was not going to work. Political values are not universal. Better to concentrate on keeping our own.

On January 18, 1930, Garrett was shot. He was in New York at a high-class speakeasy—this was during Prohibition—called Chez Madelon. He was having dinner with a young woman who worked in advertising, and with another couple. He had been married twice by then, and divorced twice. He was 51.

Two masked gunmen barged in. "Ladies and Gentlemen," one announced, "Stay where you are and keep your seats."

Garrett stood up, hands in pockets, and advanced. Here is one newspaper's account:

"'What's this?' exclaimed the writer, in a tone that conveyed nothing except the utmost peevishness. He acted like a man bored, vexed and annoyed...

"'Oh, What's this? What's this all about?' he repeated in the same exasperated voice...[like] an irritable executive who had just been hit by an office boy's paper wad.

"Mr. Garrett refused to take the pistol seriously. He was still advancing with an expression of contempt on his face...when the bandit pulled the trigger."

Four shots rang out. Garrett was hit in the hip, lung and shoulder with steel-jacketed .25 caliber rounds, one of them grazing his windpipe. Thereafter he spoke with a rasp.

The robbers fled. The police called it a bungled holdup, but not before a detective insisted on questioning Garrett on a theory that it was a crime of passion. That made Garrett so angry that he threw at the cop's head what is described by various newspapers as a dish, a porcelain cup or a small spittoon.

Commenting on the restaurant, Garrett said, "You get a wonderful dinner at this place, but it costs like the mischief."

Garrett is today classified as part of the Old Right, a name given later to those who opposed the New Deal and World War II. Some were famous, such as the critic and satirist H.L. Mencken, founder of the magazine *American Mercury*. Others included Robert McCormick, publisher of *The Chicago Tribune*; John T. Flynn, author of *The Roosevelt Myth* (1948) and a leader in the America First Committee; and various Republicans, particularly Sen. Robert Taft.

Professionally, Garrett was closest to the small band of believers in free-market economics: Leonard Read, founder of the Foundation for Economic Education; Henry Hazlitt, author of *Economics in One Lesson* (1946); Ludwig von Mises, who had demonstrated in 1920 that socialism had no method of economic calculation; and Mises' pupil, F.A.

Hayek, who would later win the Nobel prize in economics and inspire Margaret Thatcher.

Garrett's political soulmate was a literary figure, Rose Wilder Lane. She was the ghostwriter of the *Little House on the Prairie* books, working from outlines done by her mother, Laura Ingalls Wilder. Garrett had met Lane on the Atlantic steamer *Leviathan* in 1923, after his second divorce. In the summer of 1935 he and she went for a two-week drive through Midwest farm country.

William Holtz recounts in his biography, *The Ghost in the Little House* (1993): "She was nearing fifty now, he seven years older—short, fat and balding, with a voice husky from an old bullet would and missing some fingers as well... In this bed of sympathetic principle, something like love bloomed, crusty and irritable on his side, quietly supplicating on hers."

Their correspondence, preserved in the Herbert Hoover Presidential Library, is revealing, particularly of Garrett. Lane was a right-wing anarchist, more radical than Garrett, but he was the one who wrote forceful and emotional letters.

On individualism he wrote: "In principle I believe that the less we act upon the lives of others for good or evil—the less the better. Each one saves himself or he is not saved."

In the midst of the Depression, he wrote: "I'm buying a small press on which, when the worst comes, I can print a paper of my own. I learned it when I was a printer's devil. I can set type and run a press. Do you want a job? I could teach you the trade in a few weeks...For the name of my paper what would you think of Cross Roads. Owned, edited and printed by me. Advertising rates: none."

A few months later he wrote: "I'm converting an old Model A into a power plant, setting up a saw rig, tinkering. There is nothing I can think of more satisfactory, by the way, than feeding wood into a buzz saw. It's good for the dumb rankles."

Garrett told Lane of how he talked to his neighbors about the Townsend Plan, a home-grown progenitor of Social Security. He wrote, "In my folly I was trying to prove to them that the Townsend Plan would wreck the economic scheme. What did they care about the economic scheme? They would be dead before the result. Meanwhile, $200 a month. Do you see the trouble—I was right and they were right. So with the New Deal. For those who want that kind of world it is right. For those who don't want that kind of world it is wrong. And, again, it simply isn't arguable."

The letters hint strongly of an affair. Garrett wrote her: "Do you know the fish,—the shell fish,—that has only half a shell and lives against a cliff for the other half? I can pronounce it and so can you, the name, I mean, but I cannot spell it and neither can you, unless you remember it from a bill of fare, which doesn't prove it to be right. I cling to the cliff. Only two things can pry me off. One is death and the other is a female. That is why I hate females. I know what this strange fish is thinking. He wonders why anybody would want to pry him loose, that is, he wonders why anybody would him to eat. It is a weak fish. The only strength he has is his weakness, his half-shellness, his incompleteness. He is tough and to the refined taste coarse, but these qualities, which should be somewhat in his protection, are of no use whatever because when they are discovered it is too late, for him and for everyone else. When he dies he drops into the sea, and it was a hell of a little to have lived for, and he can't help it…

"Life is an ass. I've told you that. It is so in all senses, personal and impersonal."

"What do I want you to do? Nothing. You are not that kind of shell fish. And if you were, what would be the use of sticking side by side to a sea cliff? And for all this I'm in a great rage at you. If we were in the kitchen I'd throw a plate at your head."

He wrote, "Rose dear, it is more than I can understand. You shake me in the fixed principle of my life. I am angry

and happy. We two! We ought to be in a row boat somewhere in the middle of the Pacific or on a distant island. I
want to see you and yet I dread it."

The correspondence breaks off in 1939 and starts up in
1953 with a less familiar tone. Garrett remarried in 1947
and stayed married. He never had children.

The three essays in this book are written late in Garrett's
life. They are a summation of his belief that his country had
taken the wrong road.

The title essay, "Ex America," is the overview. It covers
the transformation of America in the first half of the century, beginning with the early radicals who "dine on fine
plate and denounced success." Here is the story of the
income tax amendment ("Only the intellectuals knew what
it meant"), war, FDR, the repudiation of gold, war again,
inflation, foreign aid and war again.

Viewing the world in 1950, with its atomic bomb, "octopean government" and "dim-out of the individual," Garrett
asks: would the Americans of 1900 have wanted it? No.
They would not. "Then how do you account for the fact
that everything that has happened...has taken place with
their consent?" He later writes, "More accurately, first it
happened and then they consented."

The most oft-quoted of these essays is his attack on the
New Deal, "The Revolution Was." It is dated 1938, though
there are references in it—Quisling, for instance—that
could only have come after that. It was obviously too radical for the *Saturday Evening Post*. Garrett smuggled pieces
of it into the *Post*—his quotation from Aristotle about "revolution within the form" begins an editorial in the *Post* of
October 26, 1940. But it was not until two years after he
was forced out of the *Post* and effectively blacklisted for his
anti-FDR, America First views, that he found a publisher,
The Caxton Printers. Caxton published "The Revolution
Was" in 1944, "Ex America" in 1951 and "Rise of Empire"
in 1952, and combined them in 1953 as *The People's*

Pottage.

What makes "The Revolution Was" so radical is not mainly its argument. It is its language. Such phrases as "capturing the seat of power" and "mobilizing by propaganda the forces of hatred" suggest a Bolshevik revolution. We do not speak this way of the Democratic Party, because it does not fit that party today. The Democrats' (and Republicans') main concern today is to defend and administer a territory already in their hands. It was the task of the New Dealers to capture it.

Which they did. And in doing so, they scared people.

Three months before the election of 1936, in which Roosevelt won 62 percent of the vote, the Gallup Poll asked, "Do you believe the acts and policies of the Roosevelt Administration may lead to dictatorship?" By today's standards it is a bizarre question. And 45 percent said yes.

FDR was a divisive man. People loved him or hated him. History has largely been written by those who loved him, but there was another view, and not held only by troglodytes.

Here is one example of many: Liberal columnist Walter Lippman declared in the *New York Herald Tribune* of May 22, 1937, a few weeks after the Supreme Court made peace with the New Deal, that Roosevelt was creating "personal government beyond anything contemplated in our Constitution or in any other constitution of a free people." He continued, "and it can lead only, like all other personal government in the past, from arbitrariness through confusion to tyranny." Lippmann allowed that one may argue about this or that New Deal law, but "if we look at it as a whole we must be startled to the extent to which the restraints of free government are being destroyed."

We remember the wartime Roosevelt, those image still may be found in our coin purses. We forget the New Deal Roosevelt and his digs at the achievers of the private sector as "money changers," "brigands" and "economic royalists."

We forget that in many places (including my home state, Washington) the New Dealers worked openly with communists, and that the government had to be cleansed of communists after the New Deal was over.

Garrett's economic and political take on the 1930s may be read in *Salvos Against the New Deal* (Caxton, 2002). In "The Revolution Was," Garrett puts economics aside and makes a purely political argument. The acts of the New Deal, a riddle as economics, formed a pattern as politics: they consistently increased government power. In the *Post* of February 29, 1936, he wrote: "Such a policy, impossible to acknowledge, would involve many inconsistencies of immediate policy, because the peaceable course to the seizure of great political power is a zigzag path."

After the New Deal came the debate over America's entry into World War II. Garrett argued that the unstated destination of Roosevelt's path was America as an imperial power. (For his arguments, see Caxton's 2003 collection, *Defend America First.*) One example is his editorial in the *Saturday Evening Post* of February 15, 1941, commenting on the Lend-Lease bill:

"The President tells [the people] that America must put its strength forth to save Great Britain, to save China, to defend democracy of all kinds, everywhere in the world, and to destroy out of it forever the principle of aggression," Garrett wrote. But to do that is to embrace "the fantasy to become moral emperor of the whole world."

Garrett wanted his government to mind its own business. This is because he wanted Americans to be able to mind *their* own business without being taxed, conscripted or killed in other people's causes. Garrett supported national defense. In 1940, America was threatened strategically by Germany, and Garrett urged an expensive program of rearmament. He reluctantly supported the draft. But he did not want his country to volunteer for a crusade to defeat the Germans in Europe. It was the same later on with Russia. Defense, yes. Fighting the Communists everywhere in the world, no.

His argument, presented in "Rise of Empire," had to do with the structure of the Republic. The Republic had been designed by men wary of a standing army. It was not designed for an open-ended, worldwide struggle. That would require a different sort of government. Domestic policy would have to be subordinated to foreign policy, and civilian concerns to military concerns. Congress would have to take orders from the Commander in Chief. As the leader in a worldwide struggle, America would have to have "a system of satellite nations."

In essence it would be Empire, and with less control over its own fate than a Republic. It would become a "prisoner of history," ruled by fear.

Fear of what?

"Fear of the barbarian," said Garrett.

Half a century later, we live in that world.

Not entirely, perhaps. Military spending has shrunk as a share of total output. Wartime price controls and rationing are gone. Conscription is gone. The Communists are gone as a serious rival.

But war is not gone. As I write, American troops have conquered Afghanistan and Iraq. They are in Central Asia, in the Philippines, in Bosnia-Herzegovina and in Haiti. They are still in South Korea.

Fifty years after "Rise of Empire," Americans begin reluctantly to recognize that their country *is* an empire, whether they like it or not. A young British historian, Niall Ferguson, advises them to get used to it.

Garrett's forebodings in "The Revolution Was" and "Ex America" appear to have weathered less well. State ownership of industry has been rolled back around the world. Even socialist parties now embrace a kind of market economy. Americans did not, as Garrett feared, "make the government the great capitalist and entrepreneur."

In mid-century it appeared that the big entrepreneur would wither away, replaced by men in gray flannel suits.

But the human face of industry is back. And in their companies, the new owners have largely kept the government and the unions out.

Federal power, however, has not declined. It has metastasized, letting go of price and production decisions but placing its hands on things more politically useful. By what Garrett called the "extreme and fantastic extension of the interstate commerce clause"—a hole in the Constitution opened during the New Deal—government now compels private employers to prefer one race of job applicants over another. It wages a War on Drugs. It decrees that no American shall sell a toilet tank with capacity greater than 1.6 gallons.

And how fares self-reliance? Better here than in Europe, but worse than in Asia. Self-reliance in the new America is not what it was.

Garrett died a saddened man.

"Those who remembered Garrett in his later years recalled him as an interesting, colorful, and individualistic person who erected a gruff exterior to protect his inner sensitivity," writes Ryant, his biographer. "Partially bald, he seldom went to the barber or worried about his appearance in general. He wore bow ties that matched the color and material of his shirts, often in vivid, solid tones. At times, he forgot to wear a tie. He wore baggy pants and tweed coats that were old and ragged at the elbows. Yet his handmade shoes were shined daily—sometimes two or three times a day for special occasions. He was stout and red in the face… Somewhat profane, he was a slow and meticulous writer. He chain-smoked cigarettes and loved good bourbon, particularly Virginia Gentleman. At home, he was a do-it-yourselfer, the type who fell out of an apple tree while pruning it."

Richard Cornuelle, who worked for Garrett beginning in 1949, recalls: "He was a small, impish, elegant man with a Gilded-age mane of flowing white hair. He dressed in tailored tweeds, wore a black Borsolino and carried a cherry-wood walking stick."

By then, Garrett was considered an elder of conservatism. "That characterization fit him badly," Cornuelle writes, "and he was more often than not embarrassed by his following. When one or another of his hot-eyed adherents came looking for him in the office, he would hide between the stacks in the library, smoking restlessly… 'What would he do,' he once asked me about one of these soap-box apostles of free enterprise, 'if he won?'"

When Garrett worked on an essay, he would read and think for hours. "Then, suddenly, he would seize an old-fashioned pen holder, jam a new point into it, and scrawl on white foolscap, often for hours, panting and sweating," Cornuelle describes. "Then he'd howl impatiently for Kelly, his secretary, and dictate what he'd written while he could still read it."

And the cave? "Once when he was near death's door, a girlfriend—Dorothy something—kept him alive by making his bed over and over," Cornuelle writes. "When he had somewhat improved, she tore the necessary pages out of the yellow phone book and prayed for his survival in every church in Detroit. He told me, 'You can't not marry a woman like that.' But she was an alcoholic and a pest, so he built a cement-block study near the river about fifty yards from the house. It had insulation and heat and water, but no toilet. When I asked him why, he said, 'I want to go home that often.' He called it 'the cave.'"

Cornuelle recalls sitting with Garrett "mornings on the screen porch of his house on the Tuckahoe River during his last year, scratching and yawning and talking… He was mourning a society that had first showed so much promise and now seemed so surely doomed."

In June 1954, Baruch wrote that he had reread Garrett's 1928 book *An American Omen*, which had celebrated modern management, automation and high wages. Garrett replied, "I wish I could be as optimistic now as I was them.

I am not very deaf, but my legs are not as stout as they used to be. I have just sold another book, and that means I am still going."

It was his last book, *The American Story*, a delightfully opinionated history now out of print. In *A Life With the Printed Word* (1982), John Chamberlain remembered Garrett vowing to hang on until he finished this book. Garrett said, "You can't die while you are still mad."

Garrett finished it and died, fifty years ago this year.

Cornuelle writes that Garrett left "several thousand silver dollars buried in buckets under the porch, a remarkable collection of books and a tangled jumble of papers." Dorothy Garrett, who died a year later, offered his papers to Harvard. "The Houghton Library sent a few first editions and an apprentice in library science," Cornuelle writes, who "carried away a few first editions and a handful of letters signed by such celebrities as Hoover and Baruch, and left the rest behind." After Dorothy died, Garrett's remaining papers were sold off in bundles with his kitchen pots and bed linen.

PREFACE
1953

By Garet Garrett

A time came when the only people who had ever been free began to ask:

What is freedom?

Who wrote its articles—the strong or the weak?

Was it an absolute good?

Could there be such a thing as unconditional freedom, short of anarchy?

Given the answer to be no, then was freedom an eternal truth or a political formula?

Since it was clear to reason that freedom must be conditioned, as by self-discipline, individual responsibility and many necessary laws of restraint; and since there was never in the world an absolute good, why should people not be free to say they would have less freedom in order to have more of some other good?

What other good?

Security.

What else?

Stability.

And beyond that?

Beyond that the sympathies of *we*, and all men as brothers, instead of the willful *I*, as if each man were a sovereign, self-regarding individual?

Well, where there is freedom, doubt itself must be free. You shall not be forbidden to interrogate the faith of your fathers. Better that, indeed, than to take it entirely for granted.

So long as doubts such as these were wildish pebbles in the petulant waves that gnaw ceaselessly at any foundation, perhaps only because it is a foundation, no great damage was done. But when they began to be massed as a creed, then they became sharp cutting tools, wickedly set in the jaws of the flood. That was the work of a disaffected intellectual cult, mysteriously rising in the academic world; and from the same source came the violent winds of Marxian propaganda that raised the waves higher and made them angry.

Even so, the damage to the foundations might have been much slower and not beyond simple repair if it had not happened that in 1932 a group of intellectual revolutionaries, hiding behind the conservative planks of the Democratic Party, seized control of government.

After that it was the voice of government saying to the people there had been too much freedom. That was their trouble. Freedom was for the strong. The few had used it to exploit the many. Every man for himself and the devil take the hindmost, boom and bust, depression and unemployment, economic insecurity, want in the midst of plenty, property rights above human rights, taking it always out of the hide of labor in bad times—all of that was what came of rugged individualism, of free prices, free markets, free enterprise and freedom of contract. Let that be the price of freedom, and who would not say it was too dear?

So, instead of this willful private freedom, trust the government to administer freedom, for all the people alike, especially the weak. To begin with, the government would redistribute the national wealth in an equitable manner. Then its planners would plan production and distribution in perfect balance, and thus no more boom and bust; the government then would see to it that everybody had always enough money to buy a decent living, and beyond that it would provide for the widows and orphans, the sick and disabled, the indigent and the old.

To perform these miracles it would require more freedom for itself—that is, freedom to intervene in the lives of people for their own good; freedom from old Constitutional restraints that belonged to our horse-and-buggy days, and freedom to do as it would with the public purse. And if it should be said that this increase in the government's own sphere of freedom meant a curtailment of the individual's freedom, it came to this—that the individual was asked to surrender only the freedom to starve and what he received in return was freedom from want. Was that not a good bargain?

What the people did in fact surrender was control of government.

They did not intend to do that. For a long time they did not realize they had done it, and when at last it came to them they were already deeply infected with a virus that creates habits of dependence and destroys the valiant love of self-responsibility.

The crisis was moral.

Happily for their designs, the New Deal physicians found the patient in a state of economic pain, extreme but not fatal, and proceeded to administer imported narcotics, all habit-forming, such as:

1 Repudiation of the United States Treasury's promises to pay.
2 Confiscation of the people's gold by trickery.
3 Debasement of the currency.
4 Deliberate inflation.
5 Spoilation of the savers, whose little rainy day hoards melted away.
6 Deficit spending to create buying power by conjury.
7 Monetization of debt.
8 The doctrine of a planned economy.
9 A scheme of taxation, class subsidies and Federal grants-in-aid designed ostensibly to redistribute the national wealth for social justice, but calculated in fact to reduce millions of citizens to sub-

servience, to bring forty-eight sovereign states to the status of provinces and to create in the executive principle a supreme government with extensive new powers, including the power to make its own laws by simply publishing from its bureaus rules and regulations having the force of law, disobedience punishable by fine or imprisonment.

These physicians kept saying to the patient, "Now, aren't you feeling better?" Many, very many, were feeling immediately better, and because they were feeling better and because the government offered to provide them all with economic security forever, they were easily persuaded to exchange freedom for benefits, until at last they had surrendered, almost unawares, the most elementary freedom of all, namely, the right to receive in your pay envelope the full reward for your labor and do with it what you will. Thus the Welfare State was built. The façade was magnificent; the cornerstone rested on quicksand; the moral cost of it may be reckoned in terms such as these:

If the great Government of the United States were a private corporation no bank would take its name on a piece of paper, because it has cynically repudiated the words engraved upon its bonds.

The dollar, which was long the most honored piece of money in the world, became an irredeemable scrap of paper, with no certain value.

The executive power of government was exalted to be the paramount power, uncontrollable, and the exquisite Constitutional mechanism of three co-equal powers—the Congress to make the laws, the President to execute the laws and the Supreme Court to interpret the laws—no longer functioned.

The symbol of Executive Government is the President. Actually, Executive Government became a vast system of bureaus and commissions writing 90 percent of our laws, touching our everyday lives to the quick.

The purse and sword were in one hand, which is

solemnly forbidden by the Constitution. In fact this was so. True, Congress still appropriated the money, but it could no longer pretend to understand the budgets that came from the White House and bitterly complained that it could not appropriate money intelligently. And as for the sword, the State Department, speaking for Executive Government, held that to be an obsolete provision of the Constitution which says only the Congress shall have the power to declare war. The President alone could make war, as he did in Korea.

In these twenty years a revolution took place in the relationship between government and people. Formerly government was the responsibility of people; now people were the responsibility of government.

This change was silently geared to the popular idea of Social Security, for which the money was to come from a law of compulsory thrift imposed upon the individual and a payroll tax imposed upon employers, all to be managed by a paternal Federal government. But this Social Security is delusive. In the first place, you have no surety that the money the government takes currently out of your income or your wage envelope as a Social Security tax will be worth as much when you get it back as it was when the government took it. Indeed, it is now (1953) worth only half as much as it was when the government began to take it a few years ago. With one hand it held out the apple, with the other hand it introduced the worm that was going to devour it. The worm was inflation. Secondly, as fast as the government receives these Social Security taxes it spends the money and puts in place of it a paper promise to pay you when you are entitled to receive it, so that the only security behind all this Social Security scheme is more government debt. The right way would be to meet the cost of Social Security currently by an annual tax on the national income.

Nor is that all.

As the religious apostate seems to pass under a kind of

emotional necessity to revile the symbols and images of his abandoned faith, so in the last twenty years the popular meaning of old American words has undergone enormities of semantic change and these words are scourged accordingly. The word *freedom* itself has come to be regarded as a reactionary word, if you use it to mean, as always before it had been taken to mean, freedom from the coercions and compulsions of government, even when they might be benign. *Individualism* is a word that will class you with the greedy few who wish to exploit the many for profit. The honorable word *capitalism* is anathema. Likewise *nationalism* and *sovereignty*. And the mere though of *America first*, associated as that term is with *isolationism*, has become a liability so extreme that politicians feel obliged to deny ever having entertained it. But if you use the word *freedom* to mean freedom for mankind, that is all right.

The three essays brought together in this book entitled respectively, *The Revolution Was*, *Ex America*, and *Rise of Empire*, were first published as separate monographs by The Caxton Printers. They were written in that order, but at different times, as the eventful film unrolled itself. They are mainly descriptive. They purport to tell what happened and how it happened, from a point of view in which there is no sickly pretence of neutralism. Why it happened is a further study and belongs to the philosophy of history, if there is such a thing; else to some meaning of experience, dire or saving, that has not yet been revealed.

504232

THE REVOLUTION WAS
1938

There are those who still think they are holding the pass against a revolution that may be coming up the road. But they are gazing in the wrong direction. The revolution is behind them. It went by in the Night of Depression, singing songs to freedom. There are those who have never ceased to say very earnestly, "Something is going to happen to the American form of government if we don't watch out." These were the innocent disarmers. Their trust was in words. They had forgotten their Aristotle. More than 2,000 years ago he wrote of what can happen within the form, when "one thing takes the place of another, so that the ancient laws will remain, while the power will be in the hands of those who have brought about revolution in the state." [1]

Worse outwitted were those who kept trying to make sense of the New Deal from the point of view of all that was implicit in the American scheme, charging it therefore with contradiction, fallacy, economic ignorance, and general incompetence to govern. But it could not be thus embarrassed, and all that line was wasted, because, in the first place, it never intended to make that kind of sense, and secondly, it took off from nothing that was implicit in the American scheme. It took off from a revolutionary base. The design was European. Regarded from the point of view of revolutionary technique it made perfect sense. Its meaning was revolutionary and it had no other. For what it meant to do it was from the beginning consistent in principle, resourceful, intelligent, masterly in workmanship, and it *made not one mistake.* The test came in the first one hundred days.

No matter how carefully a revolution may have been planned, there is bound to be a crucial time. That comes when the actual seizure of power is taking place. In this case certain steps were necessary. They were difficult and daring steps. But more than that, they had to be taken in a certain sequence, with forethought and precision of timing. One out of place might have been fatal. What happened was that one followed another in exactly the right order, not one out of time or out of place. Having passed this crisis, the New Deal went on from one problem to another, taking them in proper order, according to revolutionary technique; and if the handling of one was inconsistent with the handling of another, even to the point of nullity, that was blunder in reverse. The effect was to keep people excited about one thing at a time, and divided, while steadily through all the uproar of outrage and confusion a certain end, held constantly in view, was pursued by main intention. The end held constantly in view was power.

In a revolutionary situation mistakes and failures are not what they seem. They are scaffolding. Error is not repealed. It is compounded by a longer law, by more decrees and regulations, by further extension of the administrative hand. As deLawd said in *The Green Pastures,* that when you have passed a miracle you have to pass another one to take care of it, so it was with the New Deal.[2] Every miracle it passed, whether it went right or wrong, had one result. Executive power over the social and economic life of the nation was increased. Draw a curve to represent the rise of executive power and look there for the mistakes. You will not find them. The curve is consistent.

At the end of the first year, in his annual message to the Congress, January 4, 1934, President Roosevelt said: "It is to the eternal credit of the American people that this tremendous readjustment of our national life is being accomplished peacefully.³" Peacefully if possible—of course. But the revolutionary historian will go much further. Writing at some distance in time he will be much less impressed by the fact that it was peacefully accomplished than by the marvelous technique of bringing it to pass not only within the form but within the word, so that people were all the while fixed in the delusion that they were talking about the same things because they were using the same words. Opposite and violently hostile ideas were represented by the same word signs. This was the American people's first experience with dialectic according to Marx and Lenin.

Until it was too late few understood one like Julius C. Smith, of the American Bar Association, saying: "Is there any labor leader, any businessman, any lawyer or any other citizen of America so blind that he cannot see that this country is drifting at an accelerated pace into administrative absolutism similar to that which prevailed in the governments of antiquity, the governments of the Middle Ages, and in the great totalitarian governments of today? Make no mistake about it. Even as Mussolini and Hitler rose to absolute power under the forms of law . . . so may administrative absolutism be fastened upon this country which the Constitution and within the forms of law."

For a significant illustration of what has happened to words—of the double meaning that inhabits them—put in contrast what the New Deal means when it speaks of preserving the American system of free private enterprise and what American business means when it speaks of defending it. To the New Deal these words—*the American system of free private enterprise*—stand for a conquered province. To the businessman the same words stand for a world that is in danger and may have to be defended.

The New Deal is right. Business is wrong.

You do not defend a world that is already lost. When was it lost? That you cannot say precisely. It is a point for the revolutionary historian to ponder. We know only that it was surrendered peacefully, without a struggle, almost unawares. There was no day, no hour, no celebration of the event—and yet definitely the ultimate power of initiative did pass from the hands of private enterprise to government.

There it is and there it will remain until, if ever, it shall be reconquered. Certainly government will never surrender it without a struggle. To the revolutionary mind the American vista must have been almost as incredible as Genghis Khan's first view of China—so rich, so soft, so unaware.

No politically adult people could ever have been so little conscious of revolution. There was here no revolutionary tradition, as in Europe, but in place of it the strongest tradition of subject government that had ever been evolved, that is, government subject to the will of the people, not *its* people but *the* people. Why should anyone fear government?

In the naïve American mind the word revolution had never grown up. The meaning of it had not changed since horse-and-buggy days, when Oliver Wendell Holmes said: "Revolutions are not made by men in spectacles."[4] It called up scenes from Carlyle and Victor Hugo, or it meant killing the Czar with a bomb, as he may have deserved for oppressing his people. Definitely, it meant the overthrow of government by force; and nothing like that could happen here. We had passed a law against it.

Well, certainly nothing like that was going to happen here. That it probably could not happen, and that everybody was so sure it couldn't, made everything easier for what did happen.

Revolution in the modern case is no longer an uncouth business. The ancient demagogic art, like every other art, has, as we say, advanced. It has become in fact a science—the science of political dynamics. And your scientific revolutionary in spectacles regards force in a cold, impartial manner. It may or may not be necessary. If not, so much the better; to employ it wantonly, or for the love of it, when it is not necessary, is vulgar, unintelligent and wasteful. Destruction is not the aim. The more you destroy the less there is to take over. Always the single end in view is a transfer of power.

Outside of the Communist Party and its aura of radical intellectuals few Americans seemed to know that revolution had become a department of knowledge, with a philosophy and doctorate of its own, a language, great body of experimental data, schools of method, textbooks, and manuals—and this was revolution regarded not as an act of heroic redress in a particular situation, but revolution as a means to power in the abstract case.

There was a prodigious literature of revolutionary thought concealed only by the respectability of its dress. Americans generally associated dangerous doctrine with bad printing, rude grammar, and stealthy distribution. Here was revolutionary doctrine in well-printed and well-written books, alongside best sellers at your bookstore or in competition with detective stories on your news-dealer's counter. As such it was all probably harmless, or it was about something that could happen in Europe, not here. A little communism on the newsstand like that might be good for us, in fact, regarded as a twinge of pain in a robust,

somewhat reckless social body. One ought to read it, perhaps, just to know. But one had tried, and what dreary stuff
it had turned out to be!

To the revolutionary this same dreary stuff was the most
exciting reading in the world. It was knowledge that gave
him a sense of power. One who mastered the subject to the
point of excellence could be fairly sure of a livelihood by
teaching and writing, that is, by imparting it to others, and
meanwhile dream of passing at a single leap from this mean
obscurity to the prestige of one who assists in the manipulation of great happenings; while one who mastered it to
the point of genius—that one might dream of becoming
himself the next Lenin.

A society so largely founded on material success and the
rewards of individualism in a system of free competitive
enterprise would be liable to underestimate both the intellectual content of the revolutionary thesis and the quality
of the revolutionary mind that was evolving in a disaffected and envious academic world. At any rate, this society
did, and from the revolutionary point of view that was one
of the peculiar felicities of the American opportunity. The
revolutionary mind that did at length evolve was one of
really superior intelligence, clothed with academic dignity,
always sure of itself, supercilious and at ease in all circumstances. To entertain it became fashionable. You might
encounter it anywhere, and nowhere more amusingly than
at a banker's dinner table discussing the banker's trade in a
manner sometimes very embarrassing to the banker.
Which of these brilliant young men in spectacles was of the
cult and which was of the cabal—if there was a cabal—one
never knew. Indeed, it was possible that they were not sure
of it themselves, a time having come when some were only
playing with the thought of extremes while others were in
deadly earnest, all making the same sounds. This was the

beginning of mask and guise.

The scientific study of revolution included of course, analysis of opportunity. First and always the master of revolutionary technique is an opportunist. He must know opportunity when he sees it in the becoming; he must know how to stalk it, how to let it ripen, how to adapt his means to the realities. The basic ingredients of opportunity are few; nearly always it is how they are mixed that matters. But the one indispensable ingredient is economic distress, and if there is enough of that the mixture will take care of itself.

The Great Depression as it developed here was such an opportunity as might have been made to order. The economic distress was relative, which is to say, that at the worst of it, living in this country was better than living almost anywhere else in the world. The pain, nevertheless, was very acute; and much worse than any actual hurt was a nameless fear, a kind of active despair, that assumed the proportions of a national psychosis.

Seizures of that kind were not unknown in American history. Indeed, they were characteristic of the American temperament. But never before had there been one so hard and never before had there been the danger that a revolutionary elite would be waiting to take advantage of it.

This revolutionary elite was nothing you could define as a party. It had no name, no habitat, no rigid line. The only party was the Communist Party, and it was included; but its attack was too obvious and its proletarianism too crude, and moreover, it was under the stigma of not belonging. Nobody could say that about the elite above. It did belong, it was eminently respectable, and it knew the American scene. What it represented was a quantity of bitter intellectual radicalism infiltrated from the top downward as a doctorhood of professors, writers, critics, analysts, advisers, administrators, directors of research, and so on—a prepared revolutionary intelligence in spectacles. There was no plan to begin with. But there was a shibboleth that united them all: "Capitalism is finished." There was one idea in which all differences could be resolved, namely, the idea of a transfer of power. For that a united front; after that, anything. And the wine of communion was a passion to play upon history with a scientific revolutionary technique.

The prestige of the elite was natural for many reasons; but it rested also upon one practical consideration. When the opportunity came a Gracchus would be needed.[5] The elite could produce one. And that was something the Communist Party could not hope to do.

Now given—

(1) the opportunity,

(2) a country whose fabulous wealth was in the modern forms—dynamic, functional, non-portable,

(3) a people so politically naïve as to have passed a law against any attempt to overthrow their government by force—and,

(4) the intention to bring about what Aristotle called a revolution in the state, within the frame of existing law—

Then from the point of view of scientific revolutionary technique what would the problems be? They set themselves down in sequence as follows:

The *first*, naturally, would be to capture the seat of government.

The *second* would be to seize economic power.

The *third* would be to mobilize by propaganda the forces of hatred.

The *fourth* would be to reconcile and then attach to the revolution the two great classes whose adherence is indispensable but whose interests are economically antagonistic, namely, the industrial wage earners and the farmers, called in Europe workers and peasants.

The *fifth* would be what to do with business—whether to liquidate or shackle it.

(These five would have a certain imperative order in time and require immediate decisions because they belong to the program of conquest. That would not be the end. What would then ensue? A program of consolidation. Under that head the problems continue.)

The *sixth*, in Burckhardt's devastating phrase, would be "the domestication of individuality"—by any means that would make the individual more dependent upon government.[6]

The *seventh* would be the systematic reductions of all forms of rival authority.

The *eighth* would be to sustain popular faith in an unlimited public debt, for if that faith should break the government would be unable to borrow, if it could not borrow it could not spend, and the revolution must be able to borrow and spend the wealth of the rich or else it will be bankrupt.

The *ninth* would be to make the government itself the great capitalist and enterpriser, so that the ultimate power in initiative would pass from the hands of private enterprise to the all-powerful state.

Each one of these problems would have two sides, one the obverse and one the reverse, like a coin. One side only would represent the revolutionary intention. The other side in each case would represent Recovery—and that was the side the New Deal constantly held up to view. Nearly everything it did was in the name of Recovery. But in no case was it true that for the ends of economic recovery alone one solution or one course and one only was feasible. In each case there was an alternative and therefore a choice to make. What we shall see is that in every case the choice was one that could not fail:

    (a) To ramify the authority and power of executive government—its power, that is, to rule by decrees and rules and regulations of its own making;

    (b) To strengthen its hold upon the economic life of the nation;

    (c) To extend its power over the individual;

    (d) To degrade the parliamentary principle;

    (e) To impair the great American tradition of an independent, Constitutional judicial power;

    (f) To weaken all other powers—the power of private enterprise, the power of private finance, the power of state and local government.

    (g) To exalt the leader principle.

There was endless controversy as to whether the acts of the New Deal did actually move recovery or retard it, and nothing final could ever come of that bitter debate because it is forever impossible to prove what might have happened in place of what did. But a positive result is obtained if you ask:

Where was the New Deal going?

The answer to that question is too obvious to be debated. Every choice it made, whether it was one that moved recovery or not, was a choice unerringly true to the essential design of totalitarian government, never of course called by that name either here or anywhere else.

How it worked, how the decisions were made, and how acts that were inconsistent from one point of view were consistent indeed from the other—that now is the matter to be explored, seriatim.

Problem One
To Capture the Seat of Government

There was here no choice of means. The use of force was not to be considered. Therefore, it had to be done by ballot. That being the case, and the factor of political discontent running very high, the single imperative was not to alarm the people.

Senator Taft says that in the presidential campaign of 1932 "the New Deal was hidden behind a program of economy and state rights."[7]

That is true. Nevertheless, a New Dealer might say: "How could we tell the people what we were going to do when we ourselves did not know?" And that also may be true—that they did not know what they were going to do.

Lenin, the greatest theorist of them all, did not know what he was going to do after he had got the power. He made up plans as he went along, changed them if they did not work, even reversed them, but always of course in a manner consistent with his basic revolutionary thesis. And so it was with Hitler, who did it by ballot, and with Mussolini, who did it by force.

There was probably no blueprint of the New Deal, nor even a clear drawing. Such things as the A.A.A. and the Blue Eagle were expedient inventions. What *was* concealed from the people was a general revolutionary intention—the intention, that is, to bring about revolution in the state, within the form of law. This becomes clear when you set down what it was the people thought they were voting for in contrast with what they got. They thought they were voting:

For less government, not more; for an end of deficit spending by government, not deficit spending raised to the plane of a social principle; and, for sound money, not as the New Deal afterward defined it, but as everybody then understood it, including Senator Glass, formerly Secretary of the Treasury, who wrote the money plank in the Democratic party platform and during the campaign earnestly denounced as akin to treason any suggestion that the New Deal was going to do what it did forthwith proceed to do, over his dramatic protest.[8]

The first three planks of the Democratic party platform read as follows:

"We advocate:

(1) An immediate and drastic reduction of governmental expenditures by abolishing useless commissions and offices, consolidating departments and bureaus and eliminating extravagance, to accomplish a saving of not less than 25 percent in the cost of Federal government...

(2) Maintenance of the national credit by a Federal budget annually balanced...

(3) A sound currency to be maintained at all hazards."

Mr. Roosevelt pledged himself to be bound by his platform as no President had ever before been bound by a party document. All during the campaign he supported it with words that could not possibly be misunderstood. He said:

> "I accuse the present Administration (Hoover's) of being the greatest spending Administration in peacetime in all American history—one which piled bureau on bureau, commission on commission, and has failed to anticipate the dire needs or reduced earning power of the people. Bureaus and bureaucrats have been retained at the expense of the taxpayer...We are spending altogether too much money for government services which are neither practical or nec-

essary. In addition to this, we are attempting too many functions and we need a simplification of what the Federal government is giving to the people."

This he said many times.

Few of the great majority that voted in November 1932 for less Federal government and fewer Federal functions could have imagined that by the middle of the next year the extensions of government and the multiplication of its functions would have been such as to create serious administrative confusion in Washington, which the President, according to his own words, dealt with in the following manner:

> "On July eleventh I constituted the Executive Council for the simple reason that so many new agencies having been created, a weekly meeting with the members of the Cabinet in joint session was imperative...Mr. Frank C. Walker was appointed as Executive Secretary of the Council."[9]

Fewer still could have believed that if such a thing did happen it would be more than temporary, for the duration of the emergency only; and yet within a year after Mr. Roosevelt had pledged himself, if elected, to make a 25 percent cut in Federal government by "eliminating functions" and by "abolishing many boards and commissions," he was writing, in a book entitled *On Our Way*, the following:

> "The next day, I transmitted the Annual Budget Message to the Congress. It is, of course, filled with figures and accompanied by a huge volume containing in detail all of the proposed appropriations for running the government during the fiscal year beginning July 1, 1934, and

ending June 30, 1935. Although the facts of previous appropriations had all been made public, the country, and I think most of the Congress, did not fully realize the huge sums which would be expended by the government this year and next year; nor did they realize the great amount the Treasury would have to borrow."

And certainly almost no one who voted in November, 1932 for a sound gold-standard money according to the Glass money plank in the platform could have believed that less than a year later, in a radio address reviewing the extraordinary monetary acts of the New Deal, the President would be saying: "We are thus continuing to move toward a managed currency."

The broken party platform, as an object, had a curious end. Instead of floating away and out of sight as a proper party platform should, it kept coming back with the tide. Once it came so close that the President had to notice it. Then all he did was to turn it over, campaign side down, with the words:

"I was able, conscientiously, to give full assent to this platform and to develop its purpose in campaign speeches. A campaign, however, is apt to partake so much of the character of a debate and the discussion of individual points that the deeper and more permanent philosophy of the whole plan (where one exists) is often lost."

At that the platform sank.

And so the first problem was solved. The seat of government was captured by ballot, according to law.

Problem Two

To Seize Economic Power

This was the critical problem. The brilliant solution of it will doubtless make a classic chapter in the textbooks of revolutionary technique. In a highly evolved money economy, such as this one, the shortest and surest road to economic power would be what? It would be control of money, banking, and credit. The New Deal knew that answer. It knew also the steps and how to take them, and above all, it knew its opportunity.

It arrived at the seat of government in the midst of that well-known phenomenon called a banking crisis, such as comes at the end of every great depression. It is like the crisis of a fever. When the banks begin to fail, pulling one another down, that is the worst that can happen. If the patient does not die then he will recover. We were not going to die. The same thing had happened to us before, once or twice in every twenty years, and always before the cure had brought itself to pass as it was bound to do again.

In his inaugural address, March 4, 1933, the President declared that the people had "asked for discipline and direction under leadership"; that he would seek to bring speedy action "within my Constitutional authority"; and that he hoped the "normal balance of executive and legislative authority" could be maintained, and then said:

> "But in the event that Congress shall fail...and in the event that the national emergency is still critical...I shall ask Congress for the one remaining instrument to meet the crisis—broad executive power to make war against the emergency, as great as the power that would be given to me if we were in fact invaded by a foreign foe."

It is true that people wanted action. That they were in a

mood to accept any pain-killer and damn the balance of authority between the executive and legislative authority. That was an emotional state of mind perfectly suited to a revolutionary purpose, and the President took advantage of it to make the first startling exposition of New Deal philosophy. Note his assertion of the leadership principle over any other. Discipline under leadership. Note the threat to Congress—"in the event that Congress shall fail." But who was to say if the Congress had failed? The leader, of course. If in his judgement the Congress failed, then he would demand war powers to deal with an economic emergency.

The word *emergency* was then understood to mean what the dictionaries said it meant—namely, a sudden juncture of events demanding immediate action. It was supposed to refer only to the panic and the banking crisis, both temporary.

But what it meant to the President, as nobody then knew, was a very different thing. Writing a year later, in his book, *On Our Way*, he said:

> "Strictly speaking, the banking crisis lasted only one week...But the full meaning of that word emergency related to far more than banks: it covered the whole economic and therefore the whole social structure of the country. It was an emergency that went to the roots of our agriculture, our commerce, our industry; it was an emergency that has existed for a whole generation in its underlying causes and for three-and-one-half years in its visible effects. It could be cured only by a complete reorganization and measured control of he economic structure... It called for a long series of new laws, new administrative agencies. It required separate measures affecting different subjects; but all of them component parts of a fair-

ly definite broad plan."

So, what the New Deal really intended to do, what it meant to do within the Constitution if possible, with the collaboration of Congress if Congress did not fail, but with war powers if necessary, was to reorganize and control the "whole economic and therefore the whole social structure of the country." And therein lay the meaning—the only consistent meaning—of a series of acts touching money, banking and credit which, debated as monetary policy, made no sense whatever.

The first step, three days before the new Congress convened, was an executive decree suspending all activities of banking throughout the country. Simply, every bank was shut up. The same decree forbade, under pain of fine and imprisonment, any dealing in foreign exchange or any transfer of credit from the United States to any place abroad, and that was to slam the door against the wicked rich who might be tempted to run out.[10]

The second step was an act of Congress, saying, "Acts of the President and Secretary of the Treasury since March 4, 1933, are hereby confirmed and approved."

That made everything legal after the fact: and it was the first use of Congress as a rubber stamp. The same act of Congress provided that no bank in the Federal Reserve System should resume business except subject to rules and regulations to be promulgated by the Secretary of the Treasury, gave the President absolute power over foreign exchange and authorized the Federal government to invest public funds in private bank stock, thereby providing banks with new capital owned by the government. And that was the act that authorized the President to require people to surrender their gold. Congress did not write any of these acts. It received them from the White House and passed them.

The third step was a decree by the President requiring all persons and corporations whatever to divest themselves of gold and hand it over to the government. The law authorizing him to do that had fixed the penalty of non-compliance at a fine equal to twice the value of the gold. The executive decree added the penalty of imprisonment.[11]

In view of further intentions not yet disclosed it was imperative for the government to get possession of all the gold. With a lot of gold in private hands its control of money, banking, and credit could have been seriously challenged. All that the government asked for at first was possession of the gold, as if it were a trust. For their gold as they gave it up people received paper money, but this paper money was still gold standard money—that is to say, it had always been exchangeable for gold dollar for dollar, and people supposed that it would be so again, when the crisis passed. Not a word had yet been said about devaluing the dollar or repudiating the gold standard. The idea held out was that as people surrendered their gold they were supporting the nation's credit.

This decree calling in the gold was put forth on April 5. The Treasury was empty. It had to sell some bonds. If people knew what was going to happen they might hesitate to buy new Treasury bonds. Knowing that it was going to devalue the dollar, knowing that it was going to repudiate the gold redemption clause in its bonds, even while it was writing the law of repudiation, the government nevertheless issued and sold to the people bonds engraved as usual, that is, with the promise of the United States Government to pay the interest and redeem the principal "in United States gold coin of the present standard of value."

The fourth step was the so-called Inflation Amendment attached to the Emergency Farm Relief Act. This law made sure that the Treasury need not be caught that way again.

It forcibly opened the tills of the Federal Reserve Bank System to three billions of Treasury notes, authorized three billions of fiat money to be issued in the President's discretion, and gave the President power in his own discretion to devalue the dollar by one-half.

The fifth step was the act of repudiation. By resolution June 5, 1933, the Congress repudiated the gold redemption clause in all government obligations, saying they should be payable when due in any kind of money the government might see fit to provide; and, going further, it declared that the same traditional redemption clause in all private contracts, such, for example, as railroad and other corporation bonds, was contrary to public policy and therefore invalid.

The sixth step was a new banking act giving the Federal government power to say how private banks should lend their money, on what kinds of collateral and in what proportions, and the arbitrary power to cut them off from credit with Federal Reserve Banks. This arbitrary power to cut them off from credit was a stranglehold, and it was gained by changing one little word in the country's organic banking law. From the beginning until then the law was that a Federal Reserve Bank "shall" lend to a private bank on suitable security. This word was changed to "may". Thus a right became a privilege and a privilege that could be suspended at will.

The seventh step—and it was the one most oblique— was to produce what may be described as monetary Pandemonium. This continued for six months. To understand it will require some effort of attention.

When by the Inflation Amendment the dollar was cut loose from gold, it idd not immediately fall. That was because, in spite of everything, it was the best piece of money in the whole world. Well then, when the dollar did not fall headlong of its own weight the government began to club it down, and the club it used to beat it with was gold. In the President's words the procedure was like this:

> "I am authorizing the Reconstruction Finance Corporation to buy newly mined gold in the United States at prices to be determined from time to time after consultation with the Secretary of the Treasury and the President. Whenever necessary to the end in view we shall also buy or sell gold in the world market. My aim in taking this step is to establish and maintain continuous control. This is a policy and not an expedient."

Each morning thereafter the Treasury announced the price the government would pay for gold in paper dollars, one day 30 paper dollars for one ounce of gold, the next 32 dollars, two days later 34 dollars, and so on; and not only the newly mined gold in this country but anybody's gold anywhere in the world. Thus day by day the President and the Secretary of the Treasury determined the value of gold priced in American paper dollars, or the value of American paper dollars priced in gold, which was the same thing; and how they did it or by what rule, if any, nobody ever knew.

The spectacle of a great, solvent government paying a fictitious price for gold it did not want and did not need and doing it on purpose to debase the value of its own paper currency was one to astonish the world. What did it mean? Regarded as monetary policy it made no meaning whatever. But again, if you will regard it from the point of view of revolutionary technique, it has meaning enough.

One effect was that private borrowing and lending, except from day to day, practically ceased. With the value of the dollar being posted daily at the Treasury like a lottery number, who would lend money for six months or a year, with no way of even guessing what a dollar would be worth when it came to be paid back? "No man outside of a lunatic asylum," said Senator Glass, "will loan his money today on a farm mortgage." But the New Deal had a train of Federal lending agencies ready to start. The locomotive was the Reconstruction Finance Corporation. The signal for the train to start was a blast of propaganda denouncing Wall Street, the banks and all private owners of capital for their unwillingness to lend. So the government, in their place, became the great provider of credit and capital for all purposes. It loaned public funds to farmers and homeowners to enable them to pay off their mortgages; it loaned also to banks, railroads, business, industry, new enterprise, even to foreign borrowers. Thereby private debt was converted into public debt in a very large and popular way. It was popular because the government, having none of the problems of a bank or a private lender, with no fetish of solvency to restrain it, with nothing really to lose even though the money should never come back, was a benevolent lender. It loaned public money to private borrowers on terms and at rates of interest with which no bank nor any private lender could compete; and the effect was to create a kind of fictitious, self-serving necessity. The government could say to the people, and did say to them: "Look. It is as we said. The money changers, hating the New Deal, are trying to make a credit famine. But your government will beat them."

In a Fireside Chat, October 22, 1933, the President said:

> "I have publicly asked that foreclosures on farms and chattels and on homes be delayed until every mortgagor in the country shall have had full opportunity to take advantage of Federal credit. I make the further request, which many of you know has already been made through the great Federal credit organizations, that if there is any

family in the United States about to lose its home or about to lose its chattels, that family should telegraph at once either to the Farm Credit Administration or to the Home Owners Loan Corporation[12] in Washington requesting their help. Two other great agencies are in full swing. The Reconstruction Finance Corporation continues to lend large sums to industry and finance, with the definite objective of making easy the extending of credit to industry, commerce and finance."

The other great lending agency to which he referred was the one that dispensed Federal credit to states, cities, towns, and worthy private organizations for works of public and social benefit. In the same Fireside Chat he urged them to come on with their projects. "Washington," he said, "has the money and is waiting for the proper projects to which to allot it."

Then began to be heard the saying that Washington had become the country's Wall Street, which was literally true. Anyone wanting credit for any purpose went no longer to Wall Street but to Washington. The transfer of the financial capital of the nation to Washington, the President said, would be remembered, as "one of the two important happenings of my Administration."

What was the source of the money? Partly it was imaginary money, from inflation. Largely it was the taxpayer's money. If the government lost it the taxpayer would have to find it again. And some of it, as the sequel revealed, was going to be confiscated money. By this time the New Deal had got control of the public purse. The Congress had surrendered control of it by two acts of self-abnegation. One was the Inflation Amendment and the other was an appropriation of $3,300,000,000 put into the hands of the

President to use as he liked as the architect of recovery.[13]

All through the commotion of these unnatural events one end was held steadily in view, and that was a modern version of the act for which kings had been hated and sometimes hanged, namely to clip the coin of the realm and take the profit into the king's revenue.

The eighth step was the act of confiscation. At the President's request the Congress, on January 30, 1934, passed a law vesting in the Federal government absolute title to all that gold which people had been obliged to exchange for gold standard paper dollars the year before, thinking as they did that it was for the duration of the emergency only and that they were supporting the nation's credit. They believed the statement issued at the time by the Secretary of the Treasury, saying: "Those surrendering the gold of course receive an equivalent amount of other forms of currency and those other forms of currency may be used for obtaining gold in an equivalent amount when authorized for proper purposes." Having by such means got physical possession of the gold, it was a very simple matter for the government to confiscate it. All that it had to do was to have Congress pass a law vesting title in the government.

The ninth and last step was to devalue the dollar. In his message to Congress asking for the law that confiscated the gold the President said: "I do not believe it desirable in the public interest that an exact value be now fixed." Nevertheless, on January 31, 1934, the day after the act of confiscation was passed, he did fix the exact value of the dollar at 59 per cent of its former gold content. The difference, which was 41 cents in every dollar of gold that had been confiscated, was counted as government profit and took the form of a free fund of two billions in the Treasury, called a stabilization fund, with which the President could do almost anything he liked. Actually it was used to take control of the foreign exchange market out of the hands of international finance.

Control of money, banking, and credit had passed to Washington. Thus problem number two was solved.

The reason for giving so much attention to it is that it was the New Deal's most brilliant feat; and certainly not the least remarkable fact about it was the skill with which criticism was played into making its fight on false and baited ground. Each step as it occurred was defended, and therefore attacked, on ground of monetary policy, whereas the ultimate meaning was not there at all.

Consider first the logical sequence of the nine steps; consider secondly that if national recovery had been the end in view many alternative steps were possible, whereas from the point of view of revolutionary technique these nine were the imperative steps and the order in which they were taken was the necessary order. Then ask if it could have happened that way by chance.

Not even a New Dealer any longer maintains that the four steps directly involving gold, namely, the seizure of it, the repudiation of the government's gold contracts, then the confiscation of the gold, and lastly the devaluation of the dollar, were necessary merely as measures toward national recovery. In the history of the case there is not more dramatic bit of testimony than that of Senator Glass, formerly Secretary of the Treasury, who in April, 1933, rose from a sick bed and appeared in the Senate to speak against the Inflation Amendment. He said:

"I wrote with my own hand that provision of the national Democratic platform which declared for a sound currency to be maintained at all hazards... With nearly 40 per cent of the entire gold supply of the world, why are we going off the gold standard? With all the earmarked gold, with all the securities of ours they hold, foreign governments could withdraw in total less than $700,000,000 of our gold, which would leave us an ample fund of gold, in the extremist case, to maintain gold payments both at home and abroad... To me, the suggestions that we may devalue the gold dollar 59 percent means national repudiation. To me it means dishonor. In my conception of it, it is immoral... There was never any necessity for a gold embargo. There's no necessity of making statutory criminals of citizens of the United States who may please to take their property in the shape of gold or currency out of the banks and use it for their own purposes as they may please. We have gone beyond the cruel extremities of the French, and they made it a capital crime, punishable at the guillotine, for any tradesman or individual citizen of the realm to discriminate in favor of gold and against their printing press currency. We have gone beyond that. We have said that no man may have his gold, under penalty of ten years in the penitentiary or $10,000 fine."

And when the "gold cases" went to the United States Supreme Court—the unreconstructed court—the judgment was one that will be forever a blot on a certain page of American history.[14] The court said that what the government had done was immoral but not illegal. How could that be? Because the American government, like any other government, has the sovereign power to commit an immoral act. Until then the American government was the only great government in the world that had never repudiated the word engraved upon its bond.

Problem Three
To Mobilize By Propaganda the Forces of Hatred

"We must hate," said Lenin. "Hatred is the basis of Communism."[15] It is no doubt the basis of all mass excitement. But Lenin was not himself the master propagandist.

How shall the forces of hatred be mobilized? What are the first principles? These are questions that now belong to a department of political science.

The first principle of all is to fix the gaze of hatred upon one object and to make all other objects seem but attributes of that one, for otherwise the force to be mobilized will dissipate itself in many directions.

This was expounded by Hitler in *Mein Kampf*, where he said: "It is part of the genius of a great leader to make adversaries of different fields appear as always belonging to one category. As soon as the wavering masses find themselves confronting too many enemies objectivity at once steps in and the question is raised whether actually all the others are wrong and their own cause or their own movement right... Therefore a number of different internal enemies must always be regarded as one in such a way that in the opinion of the mass of one's own adherents the war is being waged against one enemy alone. This strengthens the belief in one's own cause and increases one's bitterness against the attackers."

How in a given situation to act upon this first principle of strategy is a matter to be very carefully explored. You come then to method and tactics, studies of the mass mind, analysis of symbols and slogans, and above all, skill of manipulation.

Lasswell and Blumenstock, in *World Revolutionary Propaganda*, define propaganda as "the manipulation of symbols to control controversial attitudes." Symbols they define as "words and word substitutes like pictures and gestures." And the purpose of revolutionary propaganda "is to arouse hostile attitudes toward the symbols and practices of the established order."[16]

It may be, however, that people are so deeply attached by habit and conscience to the symbols of the established order that to attack them directly would produce a bad reaction. In that case the revolutionary propagandist must be subtle. He must know how to create in the mass mind what the scientific propagandist calls a "crisis of conscience." Instead of attacking directly those symbols of the old order to which the people are attached he will undermine and erode them by other symbols and slogans, and these others must be such as either to take the people off guard, or, as Lasswell and Blumenstock say, they must be "symbols which appeal to the conscience on behalf of symbols which violate the conscience."

This is an analytic statement and makes it sound extremely complex. Really it is quite simple. For example, if the propagandist said, "Down with the Constitution!"— bluntly like that—he would be defeated because of the way the Constitution is enshrined in the American conscience. But he can ask: "Whose Constitution?"[17] That question may become a slogan. He may say: "The Constitution is what nine old men say it is." And that creates an image, which is a symbol. He can ask: "Shall the Constitution be construed to hold property rights above human rights?" Or, as the President did, he may regretfully associate the Constitution with "horse-and-buggy days."[18]

The New Deal's enmity for that system of free and competitive private enterprise which we call capitalism was fundamental. And this was so for two reasons, namely: first, that its philosophy and that of capitalism were irreconcilable, and secondly, that private capitalism by its very nature limits government.

In Russia capitalism, such as it was there, could be attacked directly. The people were not attached to it in any way. In this country it was very different. Americans did not hate capitalism. They might criticize it harshly for its sins, most of which were sins of self-betrayal, but its true symbols nevertheless were deeply imbedded in the American tradition: and, moreover, a great majority of the people were in one way or another little capitalists. To have said, "Down with capitalism!" or, "Down with free private enterprise!" would have been like saying, "Down with the Constitution!" The attack, therefore, had to be oblique.

In his first inaugural address, March 4, 1933, the President said:

> "Values have shrunk to fantastic levels; taxes have risen; our ability to pay has fallen; ...the withered leaves of industrial enterprise lie on every side; farmers find no market for their produce; the savings of many years in thousands of families are gone. More important, a host of unemployed citizens face the grim problem of existence, and an equally great number toil with little return... Yet our distress comes from no failure of substance... Nature still offers her bounty. Plenty is at our doorstep, but a generous use of it languishes in the very sight of the supply. Primarily this is because the rules of the exchange of mankind's goods have failed, ...have admitted their failure and have abdicated. Practices of the unscrupulous money-changers stand indicted in the court of public opinion, rejected by the hearts and minds of men... They know only the rules of a generation of self-seekers... Yes, the money-changers have fled from their high seats in the temple of our civilization. We may now restore that temple to the ancient truths. The measure of that restoration lies in the extent to which we apply social values more noble than mere monetary profit."

There was the pattern and it never changed. The one enemy, blamable for all human distress, for unemployment, for low wages, for the depression of agriculture, for want in the midst of potential plenty—who was he? The money-changer in the temple. This was a Biblical symbol and one of the most hateful. With what modern symbol did this old and hateful one associate? With the Wall Street banker, of course; and the Wall Street banker was the most familiar and the least attractive symbol of capitalism.

Therefore, capitalism, obliquely symbolized by the money-changer scourged out of the temple, was entirely to blame; capitalism was the one enemy, the one object to be hated. But never was it directly attacked or named; always it was the *old order* that was attacked. The old order became a symbol of all human distress. "We cannot go back to the old order," said the President. And this was a very hateful counter symbol, because the old order, never really defined, did in fact associate in the popular mind with the worst debacle in the history of capitalism.

It was never the capitalist that was directly attacked. Always it was the economic royalist, the brigand of the skyscrapers, the modern Tory—all three hateful counter symbols. The true symbols of the free competitive systems in which people believed were severely let alone. The technique in every case was to raise against them counter symbols. Thus, against the inviolability of private property was raised the symbol of those who would put property rights above human rights; and against all the old symbols of individualism and self-reliance was raised the attractive counter symbol of security.

To bring hatred to bear upon the profit motive, there were two techniques. One was to say, as the President said in his first inaugural, that social values were more noble than mere monetary profit, as if in any free scheme you could have social gains without plenty of mere monetary profit; the other was to speak only of great profits, as if in a free profit and loss system you could have little profits and little losses without big profits and big losses.

It is not unnatural for people to think envious thoughts about large profits, and envious thoughts are very easy to exploit, as every demagogue knows. But no government before the New Deal had ever deliberately done it. In a homecoming speech to his Duchess County neighbors, in August, 1933, the President explained why it had seemed necessary for the New Deal to limit personal liberty in certain ways. It was to make all men better neighbors in spite of themselves; and as if this were no new thing he said:

> "Many years ago we went even further in saying that the government would place increasing taxes on increasing profits because very large profits were, of course, made at the expense of the neighbors and should, to some extent at least, be used for the benefit of the neighbors."

Large profits as such becomes therefore a symbol of social injury, merely because it is large; moreover, it is asserted that large profit had long been so regarded by the government and penalized for that reason.

Of all the counter symbols this was the one most damaging to the capitalistic system. Indeed, if it were accepted, it would be fatal, because capitalism is a profit-and-loss system and if profits, even very large profits, are socially wrong, there is nothing more to be said for it. But it was a false symbol, and false for these three reasons, namely: first, there is no measure of large profit; second, large profits are of many kinds and to say simply that large profits are "of course made at the expense of the neighbors" is either nonsense or propaganda, as you like; and, in the third place, the history is wrong.

When the Federal government many years ago imposed a graduated income tax—that is, taxing the rich at a higher rate than the well-to-do and taxing the poor not at all, the idea was not that large profits or large incomes were gained at the expense of one's neighbors, not that the rich were guilty because they were rich. The idea was to impose taxes according to the ability to pay. The well-to-do could afford to pay more than the poor and the rich could afford to pay more than the well-to-do, and that was all.

What made it all so effective was that this was the American people's first experience with organized government propaganda designed "to arouse hostile attitudes toward the symbols and practices of the established order"—and that, if you will remember, was the most precise definition of revolutionary propaganda that Lasswell and Blumenstock could think of in their scientific study of *World Revolutionary Propaganda*.[19]

Problem Four
To Reconcile and Attach to the Revolution the Two Great Classes Whose Adherence Is Indispensable, Namely, the Industrial Wage Earner and the Farmer, Called in Europe Workers and Peasants

This is the problem for which revolutionary theory has yet to find the right solution, if there is one. The difficulty is that the economic interests of the two classes are antagonistic. If you raise agricultural prices to increase the farmer's income the wage earner has to pay more for food. If you raise wages to increase the wage earner's income the farmer has to pay more for everything he buys. And if you raise farm prices and wages both it is again as it was before. Nevertheless, to win the adherence which is indispensable, you have to promise to increase the income of the farmer without hurting the wage earner and to increase the wage earner's income without hurting the farmer. The only solution so far has been one of acrobatics. The revolutionary party must somehow ride the seesaw.

In Russia it was the one most troublesome problem. The peasants understood at first that there was to be a free distribution of land among them. When the Bolshevik regime put forth its decrees to abolish private property and nationalize the land, the peasants went on taking the big estates, dividing the land and treating it as their own; and for a while the government had to let them alone. To have stopped them at once would have hurt the revolution. And when at length the government did come to deal with the peasants as if they were its tenants, whose part was to produce food not for profit but for the good of the whole, the revolution all but died of hunger.

The American farmer was a powerful individualist, with a long habit of aggressive political activity. His complaint was that his relative share of the national income had shrunk and was in all reason too little. This was from various causes, notably, 1. The worldwide depression of agriculture, 2. The low level of farm prices in a market where competition acted freely, and 3. The relative stability of industrial prices in a market that enjoyed tariff protection against world competition.

Everything the farmer sold was too cheap; everything he bought was too dear. What he complained of really, though he did not always put in that way, was the economic advantage of the industrial wage earner.

The New Deal was going to redistribute the national income according to ideals of social and economic justice. That was the avowed intention. And once it had got control of money, banking, and credit it could in fact redistribute the national income almost as by a slide rule. The trouble was that if it gave the farmer a large share and let the wage earner's share as it was, it would lose the support of labor. And if it used its power to raise all prices in a horizontal manner, according to the thesis of reflation, the economic injustice complained of by the farmer would not be cured.

The solution was a resort to subsidies. If the prices the farmer received were not enough to give him that share of the national income which he enjoyed before the world-wide depression of agriculture, the difference would be made up to him in the form of cash subsidy payments out of the public treasury. The farmer on his part obliged himself to curtail production under the government's direction; it would tell him what to plant and how much. The penalty for not conforming was to be cut off from the stream of beautiful checks issuing from the United States Treasury. The procedure was said to be democratic. It is true that a majority of farmers did vote for it when polled by the Federal county agents. The subsidies were irresistible. More income for less work and no responsibility other than to plant and reap as the government said. Nevertheless, it led at once to compulsion, as in cotton, and it led everywhere to coercion of minorities.

The total subsidy payments to farmers ran very high, amounting in one year to more than eight hundred million dollars.[20] And beside these direct subsidy payments, the government conferred upon the farmer the benefit of access to public credit at very low rates of interest with which to refund its mortgages.

Actually, the farmer's income was increased. That was statistically apparent. Whether his relative share of the national income was increased, beyond what it would have been, is another matter. On the whole, probably not. For when the New Deal had done this for the farmer it had to do the equivalent or more for labor, and anything it did to increase labor's share would tend to raise the cost of everything the farmer bought. There was the see-saw again.

What the New Deal did for labor was to pass a series of laws the purpose of which was to give organized labor the advantage in its bargaining with the employer. As these laws were construed and enforced they did principally three things. They delivered to organized labor a legal monopoly of the labor supply; they caused unionism to become in fact compulsory, and they made it possible for unions to practice intimidation, coercion, and violence with complete immunity, provided only it was all in the way of anything that might be called a labor dispute. The underlying idea was that with this power added to it, together with a minimum wage and hour act that made overtime a way of fattening the pay envelope, organized labor could very well by its own exertions increase its share of the national income enough to equal or to overcome the farmer's new advantage. And this, organized labor proceeded forthwith to do.

But there was at the same time an indirect subsidy to organized labor much greater than the direct subsidy paid to the farmer. Federal expenditures for work relief, amounting in the average to more than two billions a year, must be regarded as a subsidy to organized labor. The effect was to keep eight or ten million men off the labor market, where their competition for jobs would have been bound to break the wage structure. Thus union labor's monopoly of the labor supply was protected.[21]

Both the subsidies to agriculture and those to labor came out of the United States Treasury, and since the money had to be borrowed by the government and added to the public debt, you would hardly say the solution was either perfect or permanent. But from the point of view of revolutionary techniques that did not matter, provided certain other and more important ends were gained. What would those other ends be? One would be the precedent of making the Federal government divider of the national income; another would be to make both the farmer and the union wage earner dependent upon the government—the farmer for his income and union labor for its power. Neither the farmer who takes income from the government nor the union wage earner who accepts from the government a grant of power is thereafter free.

Problem Five

What To Do With Business—Whether to Liquidate or Shackle It.

There was a Director of the Budget who was not at heart a New Dealer.[22] One day he brought to the President the next annual budget—the one of which the President afterward said: "The country, and I think most of Congress, did not fully realize the large sums which would be expended by the government this year and next, nor did they realize the great amount the Treasury would have to borrow."

At the end of his work the Director of the Budget had written a paragraph saying simply and yet in a positive manner that notwithstanding the extraordinary activities indicated by the figures and by the appropriations that were going to be made, the government had really no thought of going into competition with private enterprise.

Having lingered for some time over this paragraph the President said: "I'm not so sure we ought to say that."

The Director of the Budget asked, "Why not, Mr. President?"

The President did not answer immediately, but one of his aides who had been listening said: "I'll tell you why. Who knows that we shall not want to take over all business?"

The Director of the Budget looked at the President, and the President said: "Let's leave it out." And of course it was left out.

It may have been that at that time the choice was still in doubt. Under the laws of Delaware the government had already formed a group of corporations with charter powers so vague and extremely broad that they could have embraced ownership and management of all business. They were like private corporations, only that their officers were all officers of the government, and the capital stock was all government owned. The amount of capital stock was in each case nominal; it was of course expansible to any degree. Why there were formed or what they were for was never explained. In a little while they were forgotten.

Business is in itself a power. In a free economic system it is an autonomous power, and generally hostile to any extension of government power. That is why a revolutionary party has to do something with it. In Russia it was liquidated; and although that is the short and simple way, it may not turn out so well because business is a delicate and wonderful mechanism; moreover, if it will consent to go along it can be very helpful. Always in business there will be a number, indeed, an astonishing number, who would sooner conform that resist, and besides these there will be always a few more who may be called the Quislings of capitalism.[23] Neither Hitler nor Mussolini ever attempted to liquidate business. They only deprived it of its power and made it serve.

How seriously the New Deal may have considered the possibility of liquidating business we do not know. Its decision, at any rate, was to embrace the alternative; and the alternative was to shackle it.

In his second annual message to Congress the President

said: "In the past few months, as a result of our action, we have demanded of many citizens that they surrender certain licenses to do as they please in their business relationships, but we have asked this in exchange for the protection which the State can give against exploitation by their fellow men or by combinations of their fellow men."

Not even business would be asked to surrender its liberties for nothing. What was it going to receive in exchange? Protection against itself, under the eye of the Blue Eagle.

That did not last. The Blue Eagle came and went. Gen. Hugh Johnson, the stormy administrator of NRA, said afterward that it was already dying when the Supreme Court cut off its head.[24] Yet business was not unshackled. After all, one big shackle for all business was clumsy and unworkable. There were better ways.

Two years later the President was saying to Congress: "In thirty-four months we have built up new instruments of public power." Who had opposed this extension of government power? He asked the question and answered it. The unscrupulous, the incompetent, those who represented entrenched greed—only these had opposed it. Then he said: "In the hands of a people's government this power is wholesome and proper. But in the hands of political puppets, of an economic autocracy, such power would provide shackles for the liberties of the people."

There, unconsciously perhaps, is a complete statement of the revolutionary thesis. It is not a question of law. It is a question of power. There must be a transfer of power. The President speaks not of laws; he speaks of new instruments of power, such as would provide shackles for the liberties of the people if they should ever fall in other hands. What then has the government done? Instead of limiting by law the power of what it calls economic autocracy the government itself has seized the power.

Problem Six
The Domestication of the Individual

This was not a specific problem. It was rather a line of principle to which the solution of every other problem was referred. As was said before, in no problem to be acted upon by the New Deal was it true that one solution and one only was imperative. In every case there was some alternative. But it was as if in every case the question was, "Which course of action will tend more to increase the dependence of the individual upon the Federal government?"—and as if invariably the action resolved upon was that which would appeal rather to the weakness than to the strength of the individual.

And yet the people to be acted upon were deeply imbued with the traditions and maxims of individual resourcefulness—a people who grimly treasured in their anthology of political wisdom the words of Grover Cleveland, who vetoed a Federal loan of only ten thousand dollars for drought relief in Texas, saying: "I do not believe that the power and duty of the general Government ought to be extended to the relief of individual suffering... A prevalent tendency to disregard the limited mission of this power should, I think, be steadfastly resisted, to the end that the lesson should be constantly enforced that though the people support the Government the Government should not support the people... Federal aid in such cases encourages the expectation of paternal care on the part of Government and weakens the sturdiness of our National character."

Which was only one more way of saying a hard truth that was implicit in the American way of thinking, namely, that when people support the government they control government, but when the government supports the people it will control them.

Well, what could be done with a people like that? The answer was propaganda. The unique American tradition of individualism was systematically attacked by propaganda in three ways, as follows:

Firstly, by attack that was direct, save only for the fact that the word *individualism* was made the symbol of such hateful human qualities as greed, utter selfishness, and ruthless disregard of the sufferings and hardships of one's neighbors;

Secondly, by suggestion that in the modern environment the individual, through no fault or weakness of his own, had become helpless and was no longer able to cope with the adversities of circumstances. In one of his Fireside Chats, after the first six months, the President said:

> "Long before Inauguration Day I became convinced that individual effort and local effort and even disjointed Federal effort had failed and of necessity would fail, and, therefore, that a rounded leadership by the Federal Government had become a necessity both of theory and of fact."

Thirdly, true to the technique of revolutionary propaganda, which is to offer positive substitute symbols, there was held out to the people in place of all the old symbols of individualism the one great new symbol of *security*.

After the acts that were necessary to gain economic power the New Deal created no magnificent new agency that had not the effect of making people dependent upon the Federal government for security, income, livelihood, material satisfactions, or welfare. In this category, its principal words were these:

For the farmer, the AAA, the FCA, the CCC, the FCI,

the AMA, and the SMA, to make him dependent on the Federal government for marginal income in the form of cash subsidies, for easy and abundant credit, and for protection in the marketplace;

For the landless, the FSA, making them dependent upon the Federal government for a complete way of life which they did not always like when the dream came true;

For union labor, the NLRB, making it dependent on the Federal government for advantage against the employer in the procedures of collective bargaining, for the closed shop, and for its monopoly of the labor supply;

For those who sell their labor, whether organized or not, the FLSA-WHD (minimum wages and minimum hours), making the individual dependent on the Federal government for protection: 1. Against the oppressive employers, 2. Against himself lest he be tempted to cheapen the price of labor, and 3. Against the competition of others who might be so tempted. Thus for better or worse the freedom of contract between employee and employer was limited.

For the unemployed, to any number, the WPA, making them directly dependent on the Federal government for jobs, besides that they were kept off the labor market;

For the general welfare and to create indirect employment, the PWA, causing states, cities, towns, counties, and townships to become dependent upon the Federal government for grants in aid of public works;

For homeowners in distress, the HOLC, making them dependent on the Federal government for temporary outdoor employment, rehabilitation, and vocational training, besides that these too, were kept off the labor market;

For bank depositors, the FDIC, making them dependent on the Federal government for the safety of their bank accounts;

For the investors, the SEC, making them dependent on the Federal government for protection against the vendors of glittering securities;

For the deep rural population, the REA and the EHFA, making them dependent on the Federal government for electrical satisfactions at cost or less;

For those who live by wages and salaries the SSB[25], making them dependent on the Federal government for old-age pensions and unemployment insurance; *also* for stern protection against the consequences of their own personal thriftlessness, since half of what goes into the Social Security reserve fund is taken out of their pay envelopes by the government saying to them, "We will save it for you until your winter comes." And since there is no saying anything back to the government this becomes compulsory thrift. No individual life escaped, unless it was that of a desert rat or cave dweller.

It was thus that the hand of paternal government, having first seized economic power, traced the indelible outlines of the American Welfare State. In the welfare state the government undertakes to see to it that the individual shall be housed and clothed and fed according to a statistical social standard, and that he shall be properly employed and entertained, and in consideration for this security the individual accepts in place of entire freedom a status and a number and submits his life to be minded and directed by an all-responsible government.

When the New Dealers speak in one breath of a welfare economy and with the next breath bitterly denounce pressure groups, it may seem that they involve themselves in an ironical dilemma. It is easy to say: "What would you expect, since you have made division of the national income a matter of political bargaining where before it had been always a matter of economic bargaining?"

Yet they are right, the New Dealers. In the welfare state pressure groups, representing willful political action, cannot be tolerated. They will have to be suppressed at last, because in the welfare state the government cannot really guarantee Social Security until it goes to the logical end, which is to ration the national income in time of peace just as all goods and satisfactions are rationed in time of war.

Problem Seven
To Reduce All Rival Forms of Authority

The attack on this problem was progressive, with changing features, but the strategy throughout was consistent. The principal forms of rival authority were these four:

The Congress,

The Supreme Court,

Sovereign States, and,

Local Self-Government,

(for which we may take the symbol to be the County Court House.)

The Congress is the law-making power. Under the Constitution, which is the supreme organic law, there is no Federal law-making power but the Congress. What it represents is the parliamentary principle in free government.

It is the function of the Supreme Court, representing the judicial principle, to interpret the laws when the question is raised whether or not an act of Congress is contrary to the supreme organic law, which is the Constitution, and which only the people can change.

It is the function of the President, representing the executive principle, to execute the laws.

Lastly, each state in the Union has certain sovereign rights; these are rights which in the beginning no state was willing to surrender to the Federal government.

Such is the form of the American government. The idea

was that it should be a government of law, not a government of men.

In the special session called by the President to launch the New Deal, the Congress for the first time was under the spell of executive leadership and embraced the leadership principle. It did not write the New Deal laws. It received them from the White House, went through the motions of passing them, engrossed them, and sent them back to the President. That was called the rubber-stamp Congress. So long as it was content to keep that role, everything was lovely. In the book *On Our Way* the President wrote: "In the early hours of June sixteenth, the Congress adjourned. I am happy once more to pay tribute to the members of the Senate and House of Representatives of both parties who so generously and loyally co-operated with me in the solution of our joint problems."

Loyalty of the law-making power to the executive power was one of the dangers the political fathers foretold.

In that special session the Congress had surrendered to the President its one absolute power, namely, control of the public purse; also in creating for the New Deal those new instruments of power demanded by the President, it delegated to him a vast amount of law-making power——so much in fact that from then on the President and the agencies that were responsible to him made more law than the Congress. The law they made was called administrative law. Each new agency had the authority to issue rules and regulations having the force of law. After that for a long time nobody knew what the law was or where it was; not even the government knew, because the law might be a mimeographed document in the drawer of an administrator's desk. When this confusion became intolerable, a rule was made that all pronouncements of administrative law should be printed in a government publication called *The*

Register. That was some improvement, because then if you wanted to know what the law was it was necessary, besides consulting the statute books, only to search the files of *The Register.*

In the next regular session of Congress the spell began to break, and ever since, with increasing anxiety, it has been running after the power and prestige it surrendered. But the minute it began to do that, all the New Deal's power of propaganda was turned against it, in derision, belittlement, and defamation; and in every struggle over principle it was adroitly maneuvered into the position of seeming to stand against the people for wrong reasons, on mere pretense of principle. The attack upon Congress was designed both to undermine the parliamentary principle and to circumscribe the political rights of people.

It is a long story, but well summarized in the report of a special committee of the House of Representatives appointed to investigate un-American activities.[26]   It said:

> "The effort to obliterate the Congress of the United States as a co-equal and independent branch of our government does not as a rule take the form of a bold and direct assault. We seldom hear a demand that the powers with which Congress is vested by the Constitution be transferred in toto to the executive branch of our government, and that Congress be adjourned in perpetuity. The creeping totalitarianism by which we are menaced proceeds with subtler methods. The senior United States Senator from Wyoming has called attention to the work of men who 'in the guise of criticizing individual members of Congress are actually engaged in the effort to undermine the institution itself.' Many of the

efforts to purge individual members of Congress are based upon an assumption which reflects discredit upon the entire legislative branch of government. That assumption consists of the view that the sole remaining function of Congress is to ratify by unanimous vote whatever wish is born anywhere at any time in the whole vast structure of the executive branch of Government down to the last whim of any and every administrative official... Over a large part of the world today democracy has been long dead. Political processes which once assured the common man some degree of genuine participation in the decisions of his government have been superseded by a form of rule which we know as the totalitarian state. The essence of totalitarianism is the destruction of the parliamentary or legislative branch of Government. The issue simply stated is whether the Congress of the United States shall be the reality or the relic of American democracy."

No one can have forgotten the bitterness of the struggle over the New Deal's attempt to pack the Supreme Court after it had killed the Blue Eagle. Nor can anyone who saw it forget the spectacle of C.I.O. strikers, massed in Cadillac Square, Detroit, intoning with groans the slogan prepared by New Deal propagandists: *"Nine old men. Nine old men."*[27] That was collaboration.

At this point the President suffered his first serious defeat. The Congress would not pass his court-packing law. It did not dare to pass it. Public opinion was too much aroused. Nevertheless, it was possible two years later for the President to boast that he had won. Vacancies on the bench caused by death and retirement enabled him to fill it up with justices who were New Deal minded, and so at last he did capture the judicial power.

Reduction of the sovereign power states was accomplished mainly in four ways, as follows:

One, by imposing Federal features on the Social Security systems of the states and making the administration of old-age pensions and unemployment insurance a function of the Federal government;

Two, by enormous grants in aid out of the Federal Treasury to the states on condition in every case that the states conform to Federal policies, the state governments, under popular pressure to accept Federal funds because they looked like something for nothing, finding it very difficult to refuse;

Three, the regional design for great Federal works and the creation of regional authorities like the T.V.A.[28] with only a trivial respect for the political respect for the political and property rights of the overlaid states; and,

Four, by extreme and fantastic extensions of the interstate commerce clause.

The Constitution says that the Congress shall have the power "*to regulate commerce with foreign nations, among the several states, and with the Indian tribes.*" That is the famous clause. Commerce among the several states is of course interstate commerce. Now, when the New Deal undertook to regulate wages or hours or labor conditions in the nation, it did not write a law saying that such should be the minimum national wage or such the minimum national day's work, nor that the rules of the National Labor Relations Board should govern all employee-employer relations throughout the nation. Not at all. It could hardly say that without first tearing up the Constitution. What it did say was that only such goods as were produced under conditions that conformed to the Federal law—only those and no other—should be permitted to move in interstate commerce. And then the New Deal courts stretched the definition of interstate commerce to the extreme of saing that the Federal government may regulate a wheat farmer who feeds his own wheat to his own chickens on the ground that if he had not raised his own wheat he would have had to buy wheat for his chickens and buying it would be in the way of interstate commerce[29]; or that the Federal government may regulate the hours and wages of elevator operators, janitors, and charwomen in a Philadelphia office building because some of the building's tenants are engaged in interstate commerce.

On the reduction of local self-government, hear the Governor of Kansas.[30] He was visiting Iowa and made a speech in Des Moines. Twenty years ago, he recalled, the county—for example, the one in Kansas where he began to practice law—offered an almost perfect example of responsible self-government.

> "We were able, I believe, to do a reasonably good job of local government. In meeting and solving our problems we looked to the state government very little and to the national government not at all. The citizens of the county knew who their elected officers were. They came and talked with us frequently. We knew their difficulties. We dealt with them across the desk, over the counter, and sometimes down at the corner drug store. They had definite opinions about the affairs of the county. They spoke their minds freely and they registered their approval and disapproval directly at the polls on the second Tuesday of the next November. There was no doubt and no uncertainty about it.
>
> Now, that has been a matter of only about twenty years—a short time indeed in the history

of people. But in that twenty years there has taken place a most astonishing change. The court house is the same. The theoretical structure of county government is unaltered. But in practical operation the picture now is very different. Federal agencies are all around us. There is scarcely a problem presented to the county officials of today which is not either directly or indirectly involved with implications and issues related occasionally to state, but more often to Federal, regulation. There are Federal offices in the basement and in the corridors on the second floor. Except during the regular term of court there are extra employees of some Federal agency in the court room. A couple of Federal auditors or investigators are usually using the jury room. The whole warp and woof of local government is enmeshed in the coils of bureaucratic control and regulation.

And that is only the story so far as county government is concerned. You know that parallels could be drawn in our cities, in our educational districts, and even more clearly in our state capitals. Let me cite just one example. In 1874 the western part of Kansas suffered a very severe calamity in the form of a horde of grasshoppers. Our state was young, only thirteen years old. The ravages of the grasshopper threatened the livelihood of many of the settlers. Upon that occasion the Governor called a special session of the legislature. It met, considered the problem and enacted proper legislation for relief and aid…and a disaster was averted.

If that same situation should occur today we

all know what would happen. It would take practically a photo finish to determine which would land first—the grasshoppers or a horde of Federal agents. The state and the county would have absolutely and exactly nothing to say about it. The policy and the means and the method of dealing with the problem would all be determined in Washington, D.C. The benefits, all from the Federal Treasury, in such manner and such form as Washington should dictate, would come to the farmers without their scacely knowing that it was about—and we take it for granted. The other day a great number of farmers in my state did receive Federal checks, and dozens of them were wondering what in the world they were for, as they knew of no payment that was due under any of the existing programs in which they were participating."

Problem Eight

To Sustain Popular Faith In A Spiral Increase of the Public Debt.

This problem has its greatest importance in the first few years. Ultimately the welfare state outgrows it because the perfect welfare state must in the end ration the national income, and when it does that, money comes to be like coupons in a war-time ration book. At first, however, the government must borrow heavily. In order to transfer wealth from the few to the many—wealth in the modern forms, so largely imponderable and non-portable—it must be able to borrow and spend, and unless people who have savings to lend believe in the public credit and trust it, the government cannot borrow. If it cannot borrow in order to spend, the revolution will be bankrupt in the preface. That is why in the second and third months, with the Treasury empty, the New Deal was obliged to sell government bonds under the false promise to pay the interest and redeem the interest in gold dollars—a promise it was preparing to repudiate.

Well, the rest is simple because the method was simple.

For a while, and to the limits of credulity, the New Deal kept saying it was going to balance the Federal budget— honest to goodness it was, and anybody who said to the contrary belonged to darkness. In July of the first year the President said:

> "It may seem inconsistent for a government to cut down in regular expenses and at the same time to borrow and to spend billions for an emergency. But it is not inconsistent, because a large portion of the emergency money has been paid out in the form of sound loans which will be repaid to the Treasury over a period of years; and to cover the rest of the emergency money we have imposed taxes to pay the interest and the installments on that part of the debt."

If true, that would mean a solvent government with a balanced budget; but it wasn't true. At the beginning of the second year, going to the Congress with a budget that stunned all old-fashioned ideas of public finance, the President blandly postponed a balanced budget for two years, and said afterward to the people:

> "Nevertheless, the budget was made so clear that we were able to look forward to the time, two years from now, when we could hope the government would be definitely on a balanced

financial basis, and could look forward also to the commencement of reduction of the national debt."

And that was the end of that line.

The second line was a resort to the European device of double bookkeeping. There were two budgets. The one representing the ordinary expenditures of government was balanced. The other one, representing extraordinary expenditures, for recovery and so on-—hat one would have to be regarded separately for a while. It would be balanced when recovery had been really achieved and when the national income could stand it. That was the line for several years.

The third line was the idea of the investment state. The government's continued deficit spending, with enormous additions to the public debt, was not what it seemed. Actually, whether you could account for it physically or not, the debt was balanced by assets. The government was investing its borrowed funds not only in the things you could see everywhere—beautiful and socially useful things that were not there before; it was investing also in the health and welfare and future happiness of the whole people. If there was any better investment that that, or one likely in time to pay greater dividends, what was it? In a while that line wore out, and although it was never abandoned it was superseded.

The fourth line was a doctrine invented and promulgated by New Deal economists—the doctrine of perpetual unlimited public debt. What difference did it make how big the debt was? It was not at all like a debt owing to foreign creditors. It was something we owed only to ourselves. To pay it or not to pay it meant only to shift or not to shift money from one pocket to another. Any anyhow, if we should really want to pay it, the problem would be solved by a rise in the national income.

Many infuriated people wasted their time opposing this doctrine as an economic fallacy. But whether it was a fallacy or not would be entirely a question of the point of view. From the point of view of what the New Deal has called the fetish of solvency it was a fallacy. But from the point of view of scientific revolutionary techniques it was perfectly sound, even orthodox. From that point of view you do not regard public debt as a problem of public finance. You think of it only in relation to ends. A perpetual and unlimited debt represents deficit spending as a social principle. It means a progressive redistribution of wealth by will of government until there is no more fat to divide; after that comes a level rationing of the national income. It means in the end the cheapening of money and then inflation, whereby the middle class is economically murdered in its sleep. In the arsenal of revolution the perfect weapon is inflation.

(And all of that was before the war, even before the beginning of the defense program.)

Problem Nine
To Make Government the Great Capitalist and Enterpriser

Before coming to regard the problem let us examine a term the economists use. They speak of capital formation. What is that? It is the old, old thing of saving.

If you put a ten-dollar bill under the rug instead of spending it, that is capital formation. It represents ten dollars' worth of something that might have been immediately consumed, but wasn't.

If you put the ten-dollar bill in the bank, that is better. Hundreds doing likewise make a community pool of savings, and that is capital formation. Then thousands of community pools, like springs, feed larger pools in the cities and financial centers. If a corporation invests a part of its profit in new equipment or puts it into the bank as a reserve fund, that is in either case capital formation. In a good year before the war the total savings of the country would be ten or twelve billions, held largely in the custody of the banking system, represented the credit reservoir. Anybody with proper security to pledge could borrow from the reservoir to extend his plant, start a new enterprise, build a house, or what not. Thus the private capital system works when it works freely.

Now regard the credit reservoir as a lake fed by thousands of little community springs, and at the same time assume the point of view of a government hostile to the capitalistic system of free private enterprise. You see at once that the lake is your frustration. Why? Because so long as the people have the lake and control their own capital and can do with it as they please, the government's power of enterprise will be limited, and limited either for want of capital or by the fact that private enterprise can compete with it.

So you will want to get rid of the lake.

But will you attack the lake itself? No; because even if you should pump it dry, even if you should break down the retaining hills and spill it empty, still it would appear again, either there or in another place, provided the springs continued to flow. But if you can divert the water of the springs—if you can divert it from the lake controlled by the people to one controlled by the government, then the people's lake will dry up and the power of enterprise will pass to government. And that is what was taking place.

By taxing payrolls under the Social Security law of compulsory thrift and taking the money to Washington instead of letting the people save it for themselves; by taxing profits and capital gains in a system that is, or was, a profit-and-loss system; by having its own powerful financial agencies with enormous revolving funds, the Reconstruction Finance Corporation being incomparably the great banking institution in the world[31]; by its power to command the country's private bank resources as a preferred borrower, and by its absolute ownership of more than twenty billions of gold, which may be one-half of all the monetary gold in the world, the Federal government's power of capital formation became greater than that of Wall Street, greater than that of industry, greater than that of all American private finance. This was an entirely new power. As the government acquired it, so passed to the government the ultimate power of initiative. It passed from private capitalism to capitalistic government. The government became the great capitalist and enterpriser. Unconsciously business concedes the fact when it talks of a mixed economy, even accepts it as inevitable. A mixed economy is one in which private enterprise does what it can and government does the rest.

While this great power of capital formation was passing to the government the New Deal's economic doctors put forth two ideas, and the propagandists implanted them in popular imagination. One was the idea that what we were facing for the first time in our history was a static economy. The grand adventure was finished. They made believe to prove this with charts and statistics. It might be true. No one could prove that it wasn't, because all future belongs to faith. The effect of this, of course, was to discourage the spirit of private enterprise.

The other idea was that people were saving too much; their reservoir was full and running over, and they were making no use of their own capital because the spirit of enterprise had weakened in them. There was actually a propaganda against thrift, the moral being that if the people would not employ their own capital the government was obliged to borrow it and spend it for them.

Conclusion

So it was that a revolution took place within the form. Like the hagfish, the New Deal entered the old form and devoured its meaning form within. The revolutionaries were inside; the defenders were outside. A government that had been supported by the people and so controlled by the people became one that supported the people and so controlled them. Much of it is irreversible. That is true because habits of dependence are much easier to form that to break. Once the government, on ground of public policy, has assumed the responsibility to provide people with buying power when they are in want of it, or when they are unable to provide themselves with enough of it, according to a minimum proclaimed by government, it will never be the same again.

All of this is said by one who believes that people have an absolute right to any form of government they like, even to an American welfare state, with status in place of freedom, if that is what they want. The first of all objections to the New Deal is neither political nor economic. It is moral.

Revolution by scientific technique is above morality. It makes no distinction between means that are legal and means that are illegal. There was a legal and honest way to bring about a revolution, even to tear up the Constitution, abolish it, or write a new one in its place. Its own words and promises meant as little to the New Deal as its oath to support the Constitution. In a letter to a member of the House Ways and Means Committee, urging a new law he wanted, the President said:

"I hope your committee will not permit doubt
as to Constitutionality, however reasonable, to
block the suggested legislation."[32]

Its cruel and cynical suspicion of any motive but its own
was a reflection of something it knew about itself. Its voice
was the voice of righteousness; its methods therefore were
more dishonest than the simple ways of corruption.

*"When we see a lot of framed timers, different portions
of which we know have been gotten out at different times
and places, and by different workmen...and when we see
those timbers joined together, and see that they exactly
make the frame of a house or a mill, all the tenons and mor-
tises exactly fitting, and all the lengths and proportions of
the different pieces exactly adapted to their respective
places, and not a piece too many or too few...in such a case
we find it impossible not to believe that...all understood
one another from the beginning, and all worked upon a
common plan or draft, drawn up before the first blow was
struck."*—Abraham Lincoln, deducing from objective evidence the blueprint of a political plot to save the institution
of slavery.[33]

Ex America
1951

One

The winds that blow our billions away return burdened with themes of scorn and dispraise. There is a little brat wind that keeps saying: "But you are absurd, you Americans, like the rich, fat boy from the big house who is tolerated while he spends his money at the drugstore and then gets chased home with mud on his clothes. He is bewildered and hurt, and yet he wants so much to be liked that he does it again the next day. But this is parable and you are probably to stupid to get it. If you do, you won't believe it, and so no harm is done. You will come again tomorrow."

Another wind says: "You worship success, you Americans. You have thereby ruined all your spiritual and moral values, such as they were. Your controlling idea is Babylon for the masses. Since success is your idol you are unable to understand the souls of other people or that they have souls. You are unable to comprehend the spiritual content of communism and are deluded to think you can shoot it out of the world."

How shall one answer insulting winds? You do not assert your possession of spiritual values. But as for success, we may be sure that if it seems to be acclaimed here more than anywhere else that is only because it is magnificent here and multiples the satisfactions of common life in a manner that is the envy of the whole world. Having lived the most fabulous success story in the history of the human race, we are rich—so rich that the next richest country is by comparison poor. In a world where one-third of humanity barely subsists on the poverty level, this is a fact that cannot be forgiven. Yet one may be permitted to suggest that its magnitude is not the only unique fact about American wealth.

Firstly, we made it all for ourselves, the hard way, by our own free labor, and the ground of it was a life of Puritan thrift, self-discipline and austerity, while the rich in Europe, exploiting their own and their colonial labor, lived in dazzling luxury.

Secondly, American wealth has been shared with the world. That idea is still so strange that the meaning of simple words needs to be emphasized. Never before in the history of mankind has one rich nation literally shared its wealth with others. In World War I we made very large loans to our associates, which afterward we expected them to repay only in part, but which they nevertheless repudiated, not because they couldn't pay but because it was too hard to pay and because the Americans were already too rich. And this was the beginning of capitalism's fatal leukemia in Europe, especially in Great Britain, where the movement to repudiate war debts to America originated— fatal because capitalism is founded on the inviolability of contract.

Then came World War II, and remembering the humiliation of being called Shylock for expecting to get anything back on account of Europe's war debts in the first case, we said, "This time we erase the dollar mark." That was the meaning of Lend-Lease. After the war our allies would owe us nothing. All the dollars did was to measure the quantity of things they required of us—not a debt to be repaid.

During the years of war and postwar time, what with Lend-Lease, global emergency relief, the four-billion-dollar loan to Great Britain,[1] the Marshall Plan, military aid, the North Atlantic Pact and all, the amount of American wealth distributed through the world was roughly equal to the total national wealth of the next-richest nation, namely, Great Britain.

The postwar Marshall Plan was pure giving. We said to the nations of Europe, all of them at first, including Russia: "Estimate what your deficits will be for several years, count it all up, and send us the bill." Russia and her satellites declined. All of western Europe accepted with expressions of affection and gratitude. Winston Churchill called it the most unselfish act in the history of the world. In that spirit we sent them food, fuel, raw materials, machines, and even money to pay their debts. We built new factories for them, and power houses, and restored their railroads, besides irrigation works, modern roads, and agricultural projects in their colonies. Roughly, they used two-thirds of our Marshall Plan money for restoration and the other third for expansion on lines competitive with American industry, so that they might be able to compete with us in the markets of the world to better advantage; and by the end of 1950 western Europe's productive power not only had been fully restored; it was 30 per cent greater than before the war. That was sharing. Never had such a thing happened or been imagined before in this world.

Nevertheless, a shrill Socialist wind from Great Britain says: "Now you are guilty of hypocrisy. It is not for the sake of the world you do it. It is for your own sake. You have had a surplus you could neither consume yourselves nor sell to others, and to get rid of it you were obliged to give it away, for if you did not somehow get rid of it you would drown in it. Such is the riddle of your capitalism. Therefore, instead of taking merit for giving your surplus away you should be grateful to other people for receiving it."

This hurts, coming from the British, who have been the principal beneficiaries of our sharing. And there was no surplus. It was not surplus we gave away. It was wealth; and it is nonsense to say we could not have used it ourselves, if not in the same forms in which it was distributed abroad, then in other forms, since wealth is a thing that may assume any form. It is true that our standard of living went on rising, but that is not to say it might not have advanced much more if we had employed here the wealth we gave away. Could we not use the dams and power plants we built in western Europe? Or the roads we built for Europe's colonial dependencies in places we almost never heard of before? Could we not have used our money to reduce our own public debt, instead of giving it to Great Britain to reduce her public debt on the ground that it would improve her credit? What an odd paragraph this will make in history, if it is remembered, that we increased our national debt to enable Great Britain to reduce hers.

There is a cruel wind saying: "But you are dangerous, you hair-trigger Americans. You brandish your weapons in a reckless manner. You are too ready to use the atomic bomb."

The British say that. A rift in Anglo-American policy toward Asia was so explained. While saying for themselves that they could hope for a diplomatic settlement with Red China, the British made the rash Americans appear to prefer a military solution. Soviet Russia's propaganda, aiming to fix upon us the guilt of warmongering, was thereby strengthened, and in the whole world the question began to be asked: "For all they say, are the Americans really a peace-loving people? Even though they think they mean what they say, is it not possible that their insatiable economy, to go on expanding, demands the military stimulus?"

That question may give Americans a good deal of prayerful thought. As a peace-loving people we do have a terrific war history—one war to make the world safe for democracy, soon another one much more terrible to kill the aggressor everywhere forever, and now a defense of the whole free world, which makes it impossible for us to stay out of war anywhere, the bones of Nevada cracking under the stress of experimental atomic bomb explosions—and the economy expanding all the time.

But there is another history that belongs to us too, and it is more significant because it represents the activity of our own free will.

After World War I we had incomparably the greatest navy in the world. What any other country might have done with it need not be suggested. What did we do with it? We called the Washington Conference on naval disarmament and made there the only forthright proposal for real disarmament that was ever heard.

We said to the other naval powers of the world: "Look, ours is by far the longest sword. Measure it. This is what we propose. We will break our sword to the length of the next longest one, if everyone will agree to stop there. That will end the mad armament race, in which as you well know we have the unlimited advantage. None of you can hope to overtake us. We can build a navy twice as big, three times as big, and we will do it if necessary."

Was that the voice of a peace-loving people? The other naval powers, principally Great Britain, France and Japan, were stunned. They could hardly believe it. A treaty was signed accordingly. We towed our ships out to sea and sank enough of them to give Great Britain parity with the

American navy.

The sequel was that no other signatory power absolutely kept faith. Great Britain increased the range of her guns. Ultimately Japan denounced the treaty[2]. But the story of America at war is perhaps too fantastic, so that a suspicious world walks round and round it saying it cannot be true as it looks; there must be something very wrong with it, a global gimmick, a secret forethought, since people are born selfish and really cannot behave like that. If in all history there is such a thing as a nation engaging in two world wars and renouncing beforehand any material gain or advantage whatever, and meaning it, where is it? We have done it twice. We have helped the other victors to divide the loot among them, taking nothing for ourselves, and then we have shared our wealth with the victors and vanquished alike to restore their lives.

Yet there is a chill sardonic wind rising in France that says: "You are imperialistic all the same, whether you realize it or not. Call it moral imperialism if you like, and so beguile yourselves. You are trying to make the kind of world you want. You are trying to impose the American way of life on other people, whether they want it or not. Suppose they don't want it. Will you oblige them to choose between two forms of coercion—one way to embrace communism and the other to accept the American way of life? Are you not saying to other people, 'You can have any kind of government you want, provided it is anti-communist?' And morally wherein does this differ from what the Russians are saying—that people can have any kind of government they want provided it is anticapitalist and anti-American?"

An Arab philosopher rises to tell us that our sin is to put our trust "...far more in gadgets and in the manipulation of emotions than in the truth and potency of ideas. The idea of taking a college degree, getting married and settled, rearing a family, having a dependable job, making lots of money and having a solid and ever-expanding bank account—this ideal, conceived purely in those terms, is not good enough." We are so chagrined by this description of the futility and boredom of the life we live as to forget that what the East desperately wants and thinks we should help her to achieve is a higher standard of material living.

The Arab says we shall be like that until we learn to go out of ourselves to a region of joy" ...where it is more blessed to give than to receive."

This to a nation that has never had a chance to receive, only to give; to a nation that is, incredibly, for all the rest of the world, a charitable organization. This we forget and say instead, "Hear! Hear! It is wisdom from the East."

The Arab continues that as it contemplates the values of the West "...Asia—if I must be frank with you—is not impressed. In fact, despite all her darkness and misery, Asia can still do better."

Well, these Americans have not swallowed the sun. The Asians have exactly as much of it as we have. If they can do better, why don't they do it? Why do they demand our help? With our share of the sun we have aimed only to make the kind of life we wanted, and we did it all on our own. Why haven't the Asians made the kind of life they want? The wealth of Asia once dazzled a barbarian Western world. What became of it? What became of the genius and will that built palaces and temples that are still wonderful as relics in the pages of the *National Geographic Magazine*? What became of the science and technology that made the first paper, the first gunpowder, the first mariner's compass, did the first printing, and first clothed the body in silk? By now making a virtue of poverty and preferring its miseries to the boredom of good living, the Asians may have saved their souls. If they think so it is not arguable. But for them now to be saying that to receive American wealth to improve their standard of living will not hurt their souls, whereas the giving of it may save the American soul, is too much of a strain on their garment of spiritual superiority. It rips in the critical seams. As philosophy, these winds from Asia are punk; as propaganda they appeal to the softness of American character.

Two

Since the world is people and the one universal tragedy in it is human behavior, we may know that the richest and most powerful nation will not be loved. It must expect to be feared, to be hated because it is feared, to be maligned and misjudged. Last before us it was Great Britain, whose other name was Perfidious Albion. Now it is our turn. But why should we be so tender-minded about it? Why do we suffer the censorious opinions of the world to be as sackcloth on our skin and ashes on our forehead? Why must we accept the expectations of other people as the measure of our obligation to them?

It was not always so. Since Washington—until this generation—Europe was Old World and America was New World; and even as we broke the tradition of orbital separation the feeling for it was so strong that we said our role in World War I was that of *associate*, not *ally*.

The questions we ask are new. They have arisen in our time and they have a certain history.

About 1900 began the flowering of that alien graft upon our tree of sapience called the intellectual. He was the precious product of our free, academic world—a social theorist who knew more than anybody else about everything and all about nothing, except how to subvert the traditions and invert the laws. He was neither creative nor inventive; therefore there was no profit for him in the capitalistic scheme, and his revenge was to embrace Old World socialism. As a teacher, writer of textbooks, master of the popular diatribe of discontent, he was primarily a sower of contrary and perverse ideas. Living comfortably on the fringe of capitalistic opulence, he compared his income with that of a bond salesman or a self-made executive and was moved to scorn the profit motive and trample upon private wealth.

In the academic world this disaffected intellectual multiplied by fission. One made two, two made four, and so on. Their superior manners and university passports caused them to be received in the houses of the rich, where they dined on fine plate and denounced success. Standing on the eastern seaboard they gazed dotingly on Europe, which, they said, was twenty years ahead of America in social consciousness.

Notwithstanding our "cultural lag," Europe would have been glad at any time to trade her standard of living for ours. What did that mean? To the intellectuals it meant nothing. All they knew about the American affair—all they wanted to know—was what was wrong with it. They could see only its pimples and festers and treated these minor excrescences as symptoms of deep disease. Their influence for a while was underestimated, especially by those who thought their free enterprise world was too strong to be in danger, and said: "A little radicalism is perhaps good for us. It will make us think."

And so it was that after 1900 we began to import political ideas from Europe. This was reversal. Until then for more than one hundred years Europe had been taking ideas from us—ideas of liberty from the Declaration of Independence, ideas of limited government from our Constitution, and then, though very dimly, the idea that wages were paid not out of profits but out of production, which meant that profits and wages could rise together, provided only you went on expanding production.

But now, from the intellectual's transmission belt, we began to take ideas from Europe—ideas of Social Security from Germany, ideas of slow socialization from the British Fabians, and from Great Britain also the idea of political laborism, in contradiction of the American idea as expounded by Samuel Gompers that the ground of organized labor's struggle was economic, not political. Gompers had once said that he would sooner be shot than become a number on a social-security card. A right division of the economic product, and then let the wage earner do as he would with his own; that was the American philosophy. The intellectuals represented socialism to be a working-class movement. That certainly was not true here, and Freidrich Hayek is probably right when he says that "socialism has never and nowhere been at first a working-class movement." In every case, historically, it has been first a movement in the minds of the intellectuals.

The first great turning was accomplished with the ease of a Pullman train passing from one track to another over a split-point switch. The landscape hardly changed at all for a while, and then gradually, and when people found themselves in a new political region there was no turning back.

The event was the amendment of the Constitution in 1913, giving the Federal government power to impose a progressive tax on all incomes. This idea was not only European, it was Marxian, one of the cardinal points of *The Communist Manifesto*. President Wilson disarmed opposition by saying the Federal government would use this power, if at all, only in time of emergency and yet, as we now know, the obsequies of limited government ought then to have been performed. Only the intellectuals knew what it meant. Nobody else dreamed, least of all perhaps President Wilson, that the Federal income tax would be used not for revenue only, which was until then the only kind of taxation Americans knew, but for the purpose of redistributing the national wealth from the top downward, according to European ideas of social amelioration[3].

The Federal income tax was but one tool and had not its full leverage until other turning took place. It was not until the first year of the Roosevelt era that the intellectuals achieved political power at the foot of the throne. Then the Federal government seized control of money, credit and banking, and introduced an irredeemable paper-money currency. Next, the Federal Reserve System, which was never, never to be a political instrument, became an engine of inflation, and the New Deal Treasury perfected a method of converting public debt into dollars—a process now called "monetization of the debt."

By this chain of events a revolution was brought to pass almost unawares. Many people are still dim about it. The revolution was that for the first time in our history the government was *free*. Formerly free government was understood to mean the government of a free people. But now that meaning changed. The government itself was free. Free from what? Free from the ancient limitations of money. It no longer had any money worries; it no longer had to fear a deficit because it could turn a deficit into money; the bigger the deficit the richer the government was. It had only to think billions and behold, the billions were in the treasury.

After that it was merely nostalgic to talk any more of controlling government or limiting its powers of self-aggrandizement. What had limited it before was the public purse, which the people filled. Now, by this new magic, it could fill its own purse and scatter beneficence not only at home but throughout the world. If it had not possessed the wand that could command billions at will, the story of this country's relations to the rest of the world during the last twenty years might have been very different, and indeed one might almost say that for want of dollars World War II would have been impossible.

But if dollars made it possible, still, dollars did not do it. The American mind had to be reconditioned for intervention a second time in the quarrels of the world.

After World War I American feeling soured on Europe. To President Wilson's impassioned question—"Shall we break the heart of the world?"[4]—the American people said, "Even so," and refused to join the League of Nations. In the resolve to keep out of another world war they went so far as to scuttle the ancient tradition of neutral rights and passed a neutrality law forbidding the sale of arms and ammunition to any combatant nation, and, remembering the Lusitania, forbade American citizens to travel abroad in wartime on any but neutral vessels.

Such was the state of feeling when, in 1937, with the New Deal at low ebb, President Roosevelt made his startling "quarantine speech" in Chicago, aimed at the German aggressor. This was a sign of release for the intellectuals, whose evangel of internationalism until then had been hindered by its unpopularity. They went to work for the second crusade. Both their convictions and their political ambitions harmonized perfectly with the new foreign policy of intervention.

In the orchestration of this policy the intellectuals had the drums, the percussion instruments and the brass; the administration played the string and the woodwinds. To the science of propaganda a new book was added. Never before in a free country, with no actually imposed forms of thought control, had the mind of a people been so successfully conditioned. In three years isolationist became a smear word, supposed to be politically fatal, and to say or think America first was treason to mankind. Nine months before Pearl Harbor the country, actually and illegally, was at war with Hitler.

Three

"I ask you if anyone feels that this world is better after World War I and II than it was before, when the Constitution of the United States was supreme with us and the American flag occupied first place in our hearts and minds?"

—Former Senator Albert W. Hawkes of New Jersey.[5]

The first World War and American intervention therein marked an ominous turning point in the history of the United States and the world. Unfortunately there are relatively few persons who recall the days before 1914... All kinds of taxes were relatively low. We had only a token national debt... Inflation was unheard of here... There was no witch-hunting and few of the symptoms and operations of the police state which has been developing so rapidly here during the last decade... Enlightened citizens of the Western world were then filled with buoyant hope for a bright future of humanity... People were confident that the amazing developments of technology would soon produce abundance, security and leisure for the multitude. In this optimism no item was more potent than the assumption that war was an outmoded nightmare... The great majority of Americans today have known only a world ravaged by war, depressions, international intrigue and meddling; the encroachments of the police state, vast debts and crushing taxation and the control of public opinion by ruthless propaganda."

—Professor Harry Elmer Barnes[6]

Americans now are of three kinds, namely: those who

are very unhappy about what has happened in one lifetime to their world—to its morals, principles and ways of thinking—and have intuitions of a dire sequel; those who only now begin to read the signs and are seized with premonitions of disaster; and three, those who like it.

It is impossible to say what proportion any one of these three divisions bears to the total. It is impossible, furthermore, at any moment of time to say what the people want or don't want. They probably do not know. And what they say may be so like writing on the sand that a tide not of their making will wipe it out. This is riddle.

Suppose a true image of the present world had been presented to them in 1900, the future as in a crystal ball, together with the question, "Do you want it?" No one can imagine that they would have said yes—that they could have been tempted by the comforts, the gadgets, the automobiles and all the fabulous satisfactions of midcentury existence, to accept the coils of octopean government, the dim-out of the individual, the atomic bomb, a life of sickening fear, the nightmare of extinction. Their answer would have been no, terrifically. You feel very sure of that, do you? You would have said no yourself?

Then how do you account for the fact that everything that has happened to change their world from what it was to what it is has taken place with their consent? More accurately, first it happened and then they consented.

They did not vote for getting into World War I. They voted against it. The slogan that elected President Wilson in 1916 was: "He kept us out of the war." Then in a little while we were in it and supporting it fanatically.

They did not vote for the New Deal. They voted against it. That is to say, they elected Mr. Roosevelt on a platform that promised less government, a balanced Federal budget, and sound money. Nevertheless, when it came, they embraced the New Deal, with all its extensions of government authority, its deficit spending and its debasement of the currency.

They did not vote for getting into World War II. So far as they could they voted against it. Annotating in 1941 the 1939 volume of his *Public Papers*, Mr. Roosevelt wrote: "There can be no question that the people of the United States in 1939 were determined to remain neutral in fact and deed." They believed him when he said, during the 1940 campaign, "again and again and again" that their sons would never be sent to fight in foreign wars. So he was elected a third time on his pledge to keep the country out of war.

Immediately afterward, in March 1941, came Lend-Lease. By any previous interpretation of international law, Lend-Lease was an act of war—the government of one country giving arms, ammunition, and naval vessels to a belligerent nation. Not long after that, actual shooting began in the Atlantic, but for a while its meaning was disguised. Our navy was escorting cargo trains of Lend-Lease goods across the Atlantic, under pretense of patrolling the waters, and German submarines were trying to sink the cargo vessels; the trouble was that when the protecting U.S. Navy vessels appeared the Germans would shoot only in self-defense, because Hitler did not want to attack, whereas what Mr. Roosevelt needed to release him from his antiwar pledges was an *attack*. That went on until, in October, 1941, Admiral Stark, Chief of Naval Operations, sent a message to all fleet commanders saying; "Whether the country knows it or not we are at war." And still there had been no attack that would release Mr. Roosevelt and unite the country for war. After a cabinet meeting on November 25, 1941, Henry L. Stimson, the Secretary of War, writing in his diary, defined the problem that had been discussed that day. It was how to "maneuver" the Japanese "into the position of firing the first shot."[7] Pearl Harbor solved the problem. But in fact we had already been in the war for at least nine months.[8]

They never voted for the Welfare State, with its distortions of the public debt, its basic socialism, its endless vista of confiscatory taxation, its compulsions and its police-like meddling with their private lives. Certainly they never voted for it in the way the English voted for socialism. Yet step by step they accepted it and liked it.

They did not vote for the United Nations, nor for putting the United Nations flag above American troops in foreign countries, nor for the North Atlantic Pact, which may involve us in war automatically and thus voids the Constitutional safeguard which says that only the Congress can declare war. A report entitled "Powers of the President to send Armed Forces Outside of the United States," signed by the chairman of the Foreign Relations Committee of the Senate, says: "The use of the Congressional power to declare war has fallen into abeyance, because wars are no longer declared in advance."

And to all of this the people have consented, not beforehand but afterward.

They have never voted on a foreign policy that steered the ship from the American main at the top of the world to the international shoals of extreme danger. Whereas in 1945 the American word was law in the world and the Chief of Staff could report to the President that "the security of the United States now is in our own hands," five years later the government was telling the people they would have to fight for survival against the aggressor for whom we had swapped Hitler; and that we could save ourselves only with the aid of subsidized allies in Europe. Never having voted for it, having had in fact nothing to say about it, people nevertheless accepted it as if it had been inevitable in the pattern of American destiny.

They never voted for whittling away the restraint imposed by the Constitution on the power of executive government. They were deeply alarmed when, in a letter to the chairman of a House Committee, President Roosevelt asked why the Constitution should be permitted to stand in the way of a desirable law; and their feeling for the sanctity of the Constitution was so strong that when Mr. Roosevelt proposed to enlarge the Supreme Court in order to pack it with New Deal minds he was defeated by a spontaneous protest of extraordinary intensity.

Nevertheless, since then the mind of the Supreme Court has changed. What Mr. Roosevelt had been unable to do by onslaught was done by death and old age. As conservative judges fell out, their seats were filled by men whose sympathies inclined to the Welfare State. By a series of reinterpretations of the Constitution, the reformed Supreme Court has so relaxed the austerities of the supreme law as to give government a new freedom. In this process it has cast itself in a social role. Formerly its business was to say what the law was, according to the Constitution; if people did not like the law they could change it, only provided they changed it in a lawful manner by amending the Constitution. Now the Supreme Court undertakes to say what is justice, what is public welfare, what is good for the people and to make suitable inflections of the Constitution. Thus law is made subordinate to the discretions and judgments of men, whereas the cornerstone of freedom was that the government should be a government of law, not of men.

The people did not vote to debase the dollar. Everything that has happened to money was done to it by government, beginning with the deceptive separation of people from their own gold, then a confiscation of the gold, then making it a crime for a private citizen to own gold, together with a law forbidding contracts to be made in any kind of money but irredeemable paper currency, and finally the dishonorable repudiation of the promissory words engraved on its bonds. All of this with an air of leave-these-things-to-the-wisdom-of-government, as if people could not understand the mysteries of money. That was absurd. The controlling facts about money are not mysterious. By contrast, in 1896, there was a very grave monetary question to be settled. It was silver versus gold; or inflation versus sound money. It was taken to the people, and the people, not the government, decided it. The people voted for sound money.

Enough of this history if it serves to indicate that in our time, actually in a few years, a momentous change has taken place in the relationship between government and people. It is commonplace to say that people have lost control of government. It is a thing too vast, too complex, too pervasive in all the transactions of life to be comprehended by the individual citizen. Indeed, as the Hoover Commission was able to show, the government no longer comprehends itself.

While the number of those who administer, or assist to administer, executive government has increased fivefold, and while the expenditures of Federal government have increased twenty times in twenty years, the power of the individual to resist the advance of its authority has not increased at all. In fact it has diminished. Even organized pressure groups, such as farmers and union labor, no longer resist. They ride it and use their influence to gain freer access to the illusory benefits that now flow in all directions from Washington.

Those who remember what the American world was

like in the preceding generation do not need the record. The change it indicates is known to them by feeling.

Formerly it was natural for the citizen to think and speak of *my* government; or for an exasperated taxpayer to say to a supercilious bureaucrat, "Look, I support this government. You are working for me. Understand?"

That spirit has entirely disappeared. The taxpayer who now goes on his errand to Washington is another person. He is timorous and respectful. He does not tell the bureaucrat; the bureaucrat tells him. He has the sense of dealing with a vast impersonal power, and it is power that may legally take away his entire income. Instead of thinking and speaking of *my* government he now speaks of it as *the government*, and this almost unconscious change from the possessive *my* to the article *the* is very significant. Only recently has it occurred in common speech that the government does this or that for *its* people.

In the recent great debate on foreign policy, wherein the theme was the power of the President versus the Constitutional prerogatives of the Congress, Senator Watkins suddenly exclaimed: "Someone else seems to be speaking for the people."[9]

Who else could be speaking for the people? Only government. And note that when now we speak of government we mean not Congress, and of course not the Supreme Court, but the *executive power*, seated in the White House and spread also among various administrative agencies that make and execute their own laws, thereby exercising legislative, executive, and judicial functions, all three at once.

Four

Beyond how it works and how it touches our lives, how little we know really about the nature of government. You may identify its parts and when you have accounted for all the parts you have the whole. But if you say the parts are in the whole and the whole is in the parts, and stop there, you stop just where something else begins.

The whole is more than the sum of its parts, even as what we call society is more than the sum of its members. That which is more is what Rousseau called the General Will, acting by a process that cannot be understood as a simple counting of hands. So it is with government. The whole, beyond being the sum of its parts, is a thing in itself, organic and self-creative, with a kind of power derived from the center of its own being. Almost the only philosopher who has applied this thought to government was J.C. Smuts.

In his work, *Holism and Evolution*[10], he said:

> "What is not generally recognized is that the conception of wholes covers a much wider field than that of life...and that beyond the ordinary domain of biology it applies in a sense to human associations like the state.
>
> In the human being, regarded as a whole that is more than the sum of its parts, there is a central control that becomes conscious and mysteriously produces what we call personality. This same thing happens again in a composite whole, which is the group, and then in the course of human associations this central control becomes individual in the state."

The founders of the American government knew history. As far back as they could see all governments both good and bad, no matter in what form they appeared, had certain features in common, such as a natural appetite for power, a passion to act upon peoples' lives, a will to live, resources of self-perpetuation and longings for grandeur—with always the one sequel, that they abused their power and fell and were succeeded by governments that did it all over again, as if by some kind of inner compulsion.

The founders of the American government did not attempt to formulate this law of inner compulsion. What they did was to create a government that could not obey such a law if one existed.

First of all, this was to be a government without the attribute of ultimate sovereignty, so that always in the final case the people would possess the sovereign power. Then a written Constitution to be the supreme law of the land, and under the Constitution a government of three separate and coequal powers, namely, Congress as the legislative power, the President as the executive power, and the Supreme Court as the judicial power, each of these three powers so delicately balanced that any one could check the other two. The President could veto an act of Congress, but by a two-thirds vote Congress could override his veto, and then, in either case, whether the President had signed the law or Congress had passed it over his veto, the Supreme Court could say whether or not it was a constitutional law, and if it said "no" the law was dead. In the background all the time was the sovereign power of the people, who if they were so minded could change the Constitution.

Whether or not there was an unformulated law of being that had obliged all governments before to destroy themselves by first exaggerating and then abusing their powers, there was one feature the founding fathers apparently did not see clearly, for if they had they almost certainly would have done more about it. It was a very obvious fact. No government can acquire power and put it forth by law and edict. It must have the means. A tyrant may issue laws and edicts, but if he lacks the means to enforce them they have no fury. In the ancient case, means might be the direct command of labor, foods and materials. So the pyramids were built. In the modern case, means will be money.

That is why every government in the secret recesses of its nature favors inflation. Inflation provides the means. Under pretense of making money cheap for the people, the government creates money for itself. When it goes into debt for what it calls the public welfare it first fills its own purse and then, as it spends the money, it extends its authority over the lives and liberties of the people. It suborns them. Their consent is bought. It is bought with the proceeds of inflation.

Senator Dirksen[11] tells how Cordell Hull[12], then Secretary of State, expounded to him the New Deal's doctrine of corrupting the people for their own good. "My boy," Hull said, "this follows a bent of human philosophy. At first people will demur at the idea of subsidies and accept them very reluctantly, and then after awhile they will accept them in good grace, and later they will demand them."

The root evils of inflation are political, not monetary; but, since the monetary effects take place immediately and touch people in sensitive places, whereas the greater evils work slowly, this important truth is obscured. Certainly what happens to the integrities of government and to the morals of the people is much more important than anything that can happen to the dollar.

Moreover, the monetary effects are erasable. The purchasing power of your money falls. The value of the money you have saved may be halved. The creditor class may be terribly hurt. The vast wealth represented by pieces of engraved paper in safety-deposit boxes may crumble away. And yet none of this need be calamitous provided, first, it happens slowly over a period of years, so that the many compensating factors have time to act, and provided, secondly, that the dynamic principles by which wealth renews itself are jealously preserved.

So long as the effects are monetary only, periodical inflation is intoxicating. It is the oxygen of booms, and everybody loves a boom, even while at the same time knowing better and that the reckoning will come.

All the primer sermons against inflation leave out the compensations. Profits rise, and, although they may be illusory, one would sooner have illusory profits than none. Speculative opportunities appear. Much more than we like to admit, one man's loss may be another's gain. As the value of money falls the price of assets will rise. The value of a dollar hidden in the cellar will decrease. But the value of the house over the cellar will increase. If you both own the house and have dollars hidden in the cellar you may come out about even; if you own only the house with no dollars hidden in the cellar you may beat the inflation. There have been times, as in the 1870s and 1880s, when material wealth has increased with prices falling. Nevertheless, under these conditions people are despondent and there is no feeling of prosperity.

These sayings are heretical. The use of them is to make a distinction between the kind of inflation that spells economic folly for which people themselves are to blame and, on the other hand, the kind of inflation that serves government as an instrument of policy and is intended to produce revolutionary social change.

When in the conquest of power and for political ends a government deliberately engineers inflation, all the monetary evils occur as before, and then to these you add such consequences as: *first*, that as the government expands explosively the people will lose control of it; *secondly*, as the people receive millions of checks from the automatic printing machines in the United States Treasury they learn to become dependent on government for aid and comfort; *thirdly*, people are first enticed by the benefits and then obliged by authority to exchange freedom for status; and finally, the revelry of public money which for a while seems to cost nobody anything, brings to pass a state of moral obliquity throughout society.

The monetary debacle is relatively unimportant. The moral debacle is cancerous and possibly incurable.

Five

On the use of inflation as a revolutionary weapon, Lenin said the best way to destroy the capitalist system was to debauch its currency.

Writing in 1919, John Maynard Keynes said:

> "Lenin was certainly right. There is no subtler, no surer means of overturning the existing basis of society than to debauch the currency... By a continuing process of inflation, governments can confiscate secretly and unobserved an important part of the wealth of their citizens. By this means they not only confiscate, but confiscate arbitrarily, and while the process impoverishes many it actually enriches some.[13]"

John Maynard Keynes was the brilliant John Law of modern finance. He gave the New Deal the scientific jargon for deficit spending and managed inflation, probably because he wanted to see how it would work here before England tried it.

The American who speaks most clearly on the political evils of deliberate inflation is Professor Walter E. Spahr.

He says:

> "It should not be surprising that apparently all

who would socialize our economy are opposed to the restoration of a redeemable currency in the United States. Either because they understand the relationship between an irredeemable currency and the processes of socialization or because they simply note that Socialist, Communist, and Fascist governments employ irredeemable currencies as a means of controlling and managing the people, advocates of government dictatorship seem invariably to defend irredeemable currencies with the utmost vigor. The evidence seems over-whelming that a defender of irredeemable cur-rency is, wittingly or unwittingly, an advocate of socialism or of government dictatorship in some form.

So long as a government has the power over a people that is provided by an irredeemable cur-rency, all efforts to stop a government disposed to lead a people into socialism tend to be, and prob-ably will be, futile. The people of the United States have observed all sorts of efforts, organized and individual, to bring pressure upon Congress to end its spending orgy and processes of social-ization. It should be amply clear by this time that none of these efforts has succeeded. Moreover, there is no reason for supposing that any of them, except the restoration of redeemability, can suc-ceed in arresting our march into socialism."

Here you have the devil, his convert and his antagonist, all three, bearing witness alike; and to this you add the tes-timony of experience which is complete in Russia, unfin-ished in Europe, and cumulative in this country.

Those who take the New Deal to have been the begin-ning of revolutionary change in the character of government are wont to cite its laws, and its many innovations within the law and to forget that if it had been without the means to enforce them all of its intentions would have died in the straw. It had to have money; and not only a great deal of money, but freedom from the conventional limitations of money. It knew that.

Unerringly, therefore, its first act was to prepare inflation; and this was to be a kind of inflation that we had never imagined before, that is, inflation for a premeditated political purpose.

First it called out of the people's hands all of the gold there was under the pretense of conserving it for the duration of the emergency. Having got physical possession of the gold, its next act was to confiscate it. By edict, all gold then existing in the country as well as any that might thereafter be mined became government property. Thus gold was nationalized. A private citizen, under pain of fine and imprisonment, was forbidden to have a gold piece in his possession. In place of that famous American gold standard paper dollar, which was the same as gold in the whole wide world because the holder could exchange it for gold at will, there was introduced a paper dollar redeemable in nothing but itself. This irredeemable paper dollar was planned money—planned for inflation. Not only was it declared to be lawful money for all purposes; it was made to be the *only* lawful money. Private contracts calling for payment in any other kind of money were illegal.

After that it was all coasting. The New Deal planners in the White House wrote a series of monetary laws which a captive Congress enacted, sometimes without even reading them.

One of these laws authorized the government to print three billion dollars of counterfeit money—literally counterfeit, because it would represent nothing of value beyond the engraver's art. It resembled money and the government said it was money, but the word of the government was no longer of any value since it had just performed an act of repudiation.

Another law authorized the government to help itself to three billion dollars out of the Federal Reserve banks in exchange for its IOU's. That was the beginning of the practice of converting government deficits into money.

Another law authorized the President in his own discretion to "reduce the gold content of the dollar." Here the ingenuity of the planners was superb. This new irredeemable paper dollar had no gold content. The fiction that it had nevertheless was to serve a purpose.

One way to depreciate the value of the dollar was to print it endlessly; but that was yet too slow for the planners. Another way was to price the dollar down in terms of gold. Suddenly then the United States Treasury began to buy gold all over the world, offering each day more and more dollars for an ounce of gold, with the result of making the paper dollar worth less. This was the weirdest spectacle in all monetary history. Never before has a government undertaken in a deliberate manner to beat down the international value of its own money.

How many more dollars today than yesterday should be offered for an ounce of gold was each morning settled between the President and the Secretary of the Treasury.

In his private diary the Secretary of the Treasury, Mr. Morgenthau,[14] wrote:

> "The actual price on any given day made little difference. The amounts settled on were generally arbitrary. One day, for instance, the bedside conference decided on a rise of 21 cents; 'It's a lucky number,' the President remarked, 'because

it's three times seven.'"

Mr. Morgenthau commented:

"If anybody ever knew how we really set the gold price through a combination of lucky numbers, and so forth, I think they would really be frightened."

When this wonderful bedside hoax began, the price of gold everywhere in the world was $20.67 an ounce in American money; when it ended the United States Treasury was offering $35 an ounce for all the free gold in the world.

At that point the President announced that the imaginary gold content of the dollar was reduced from 100 to 59 cents. Bad as it may sound, the planners knew all the time what they were doing. The outcome was that the New Deal got nearly three billion dollars out of the sky, to do with what it would. How? It was very simple.

The government said:

"When we nationalized the gold and buried it at Fort Knox it was worth $20.67 and ounce. Now it is worth $35.00 an ounce. The difference is $2,800,000,000, and that is profit and belongs to the government."

Later, when the Recovery Program was sagging, the Congress delivered to the President a free public purse with more than three billion dollars in it, to do with what he would.

By that time the meaning of money had become exceedingly dim. The Congress could appropriate billions without asking or thinking where the money would come from. The government knew how to find billions. It had learned how to turn its deficits into money by forcing its IOU's into the banks, where they served as security for more credit.

The national debt began to rise in an alarming manner and conservative economists filled the land with cries of impending ruin. Yet nothing disastrous happened. People began to ask why this could not go on forever. Where was the end of it? Why were all the Cassandras wrong—the Cassandra, the prophet of ill, fated to prophesy truly and be unbelieved?

Six

Here one may throw away the economic almanacs. The answer is not in them. They all alike foretold disaster. But where was it? What was Nemesis hiding, or was she dead?

How was it that after eight years of New Deal inflation, then World War II, and then five years of postwar inflation, people as a whole were better fed and clothed and housed and able to consume more of the satisfactions of life than ever before? The material content of life was higher than before the Great Depression. In the year, say, 1950, almost nobody would have been willing to go back to the standard of living that was thought high in 1929.

If this cannot be accounted for, then we live by delusion, and fallacy becomes wisdom.

In the first place, never had a crew of planners captured a galleon so rich. They did not themselves know how rich it was, and for a while they were amazed to find how much they could spend.

Secondly, it was not only that the actual wealth of the country was greater than anybody realized; the country's dynamic power to create and recreate wealth on demand was like x in the algebraic equation. It seemed to be an inexhaustible power and had always been underestimated. The Kaiser underestimated it in World War I, Hitler in World War II; we underestimated it ourselves. It was so great that the injury done by inflation to the creditor class could be absorbed, and all the more easily because there is in this country almost no creditor class as such, like the very old *rentier* class in Europe. Here the rule is that creditors are also debtors and producers, participating actively in the process of wealth creation.

Thirdly—and this is crucial ground—the inflation prepared by the New Deal was primarily political, not economic.

John Maynard Keynes, whom you may take to be the foremost modern authority on inflation, had said, as above, that "while the process impoverishes many it actually enriches some." The political meaning of that truth had never been formulated.

Well then, since inflation may act both to impoverish and to enrich, how will you plan inflation for political ends, with intent to bring about a redistribution of the national income and revolutionary social change? Certainly you will plan it to enrich the greatest possible number, for then you will have the acclaim of the people and your revolution will be popular. Suppose you can plan it to enrich, first, the farmers, who besides their vote have a traditional power to intimidate Congress; secondly, organized labor, which also, besides its vote, knows how to scare Congress, and thirdly, people in the low-income brackets. These low-income people you will call the underprivileged, and you may increase their expectations and setting for them a higher minimum standard of living, which the government will undertake to provide.

If you can enrich all of these you will have increased temporarily the buying power of roughly two-thirds of the population. And then as they spend their money and prices rise, there may be a boom in business. If that happens you may be sure that businessmen and bankers will stand halfway with you. True, they will get worried from time to time and say, "Inflation must stop." But if you say to them, "Then do you want deflation?" they will say, "No, no, not that. But let's stop it here." And they will be entirely with you when you propose to employ all the resources of government, even a little more inflation, to prevent deflation, because deflation is very bitter medicine.

That is the way the New Deal planned inflation and as the New Deal planned it so it has continued ever since.

To the farmers it gave cheap money and credit, a system of price supports the cost of which is met out of the public treasury, and a guarantee of "parity," which means that if other prices rise so shall the level of farm prices be raised by more subsidies—with this total result, first, that the farmer's share of the national income was increased, and secondly, that immunity from the evil effects of inflation was conferred upon him as a class.

To organized labor it gave, first, complete exemption from the antitrust laws, and then the legal right to create and exercise a labor monopoly under which unionism becomes compulsory and a man has to pay for the right to work. What has reconciled the individual to this condition is that organized labor, by virtue of its legal monopoly and through collective bargaining, has been able to keep wages rising faster than prices. Moreover, it has been able to get into its contracts the so-called escalator clause, which says that as the cost of living rises wages shall be automatically increased. Thus organized labor's share of the national income was increased and it also achieved as a class immunity from the monetary evils of inflation.

To the people in the low-income brackets it gave the fascinating bauble of Social Security. How to keep this bauble from withering, as prices rise and the buying power of the Social Security payments out of the United States Treasury falls, is a problem that has not yet been solved.

Either these people will be tragically disappointed, even defrauded, or the Congress from time to time will have to appropriate billions more to increase the government's payments to them.[15]

Seven

So inflation as the New Deal planned it was bound to be popular. Many were enriched and few were impoverished. Those who have been enriched perhaps could afford to pension or assist the few who have been impoverished, and if this could be arranged, and if it could go on forever, what a world this would be! The government would never have to balance its budget, debt would become a myth, and nobody ever again would have to worry about money.

Has that the sound of fantasy? Nevertheless, it is the pure logic of inflation.

Some time ago the President's Council of Economic Advisors began to expound the theory of perpetual inflation and perpetual boom. They began to argue that if creditors continued to be impoverished by rising prices, it would be better to relieve their distress by aid from the public treasury than to deflate wages and prices, which would hurt too many.

Thus immunity for everybody—immunity from the monetary effects of inflation, provided by more inflation.

What you get then is an economy moved by jet propulsion through the stratosphere. It must go higher and faster or crash. Deceleration might be fatal. The government cannot afford to balance its budget or to stop deficit spending, because its spending is the gas of jet propulsion.

For how long and how far can it go? To infinity? Certainly not to infinity, quite. Since it cannot go to infinity and since it cannot stop or decelerate without crashing, what can the sequel be?[16]

The answer to that question is already latent in the

national mind; and that perhaps is the one fatal fact of all.

We know very well what the sequel will be, and yet we go on dreaming that we dream, which is a kind of psychic device for cheating reality.

The truth of this you may test for yourself.

Many are in earnest when they say that unless people can reconquer government its bigness will swallow them up.

Ask this: "Will you demobilize government? Will you cut it back to the limited functions that were though proper to government in 1925?"

They will say: "No. You can't do that."

"Why not?"

"Because in the first place it is not politically feasible to go back. Moreover, with government now spending one-fourth or more of the national income even in peacetime, its new functions are so ramified in the economy that to abolish them would strip the gears. But it must stop growing."

Then ask: "What new function of government would you stop the growth of?"

The answers to that will be vague, desultory and irrelevant. Each new function of government has its own powerful clients and beneficiaries, wishing only for it to grow.

Many are sincere who say the dragon of inflation must be overcome, else we are ruined. But if you press them you will find that they do not want to slay the dragon; all they want is to chain it down.

Ask them—let it be a banker, a merchant, an industrialist—ask them: "How much depression and unemployment are you willing to face as the price of deflation?"

The answer will be: "It is not deflation we are talking about. We are saying that inflation must stop."

"You are proposing then to let all past inflation stand

and to stabilize at the very top the greatest inflationary boom that has ever occurred in this country?"

The answer will be: "It is better gradually to absorb the consequences of past inflation than to have deflation."

Say to them: "By your own definitions, inflation has a kind of momentum; it feeds on itself and is self-accelerating. Therefore to stop it suddenly may cause a depression and unemployment, because for the expectation of continuously rising prices you substitute all at once the notion of static or falling prices."

They will say: "That was once true. But now it is possible to stop inflation without having to face deflation, falling prices, reaction or unemployment."

"Why now is that true for the first time in economic history?"

"Because the government has learned how to intervene to keep the economy in a state of equilibrium."

There is your answer—the fatal answer latent in the nation's mind. The government will intervene. The government will be responsible.

What are these new responsibilities of government? Look at them. The government now undertakes:

1 To keep an ever-expanding economy in a state of equilibrium. (The perpetual boom without mishap.)
2 To maintain full employment in any case.
3 To provide all the buying power the people need, even by inflation.
4 To maintain the national income at any optimum level and to see that it is properly distributed.
5 To provide for the poor, the old, and the unemployed, if there are any unemployed.
6 Necessarily, therefore, to prevent deflation, which means to say that it undertakes to see that

the price of a boom shall never be paid.

Now if and when the signs of trouble appear, what will the government do? What will the people expect it to do?

It will undertake to discharge its new responsibilities. To do that it will be obliged to take control of the entire economy, as the New Deal tried to do in the first one hundred days of the revolution and as it would actually have done but for a sick chicken on the New York poultry market, which was the cause of bringing the National Industrial Recovery Act before an unreformed Supreme Court. There the Blue Eagle was killed. But what reason is there to suppose that a second Blue Eagle would suffer that fate at the hands of a reformed and liberalized Supreme Court?

What the New Deal planners tried to do was strange and sudden. What the government will do in the next crisis is pre-determined.

And when this end has come to pass not only will we be through with the fiction of free prices, free markets, free contracts, and free enterprise; we shall probably be through also with inflation.

A government that has arrived at the ultimate goal of total power may dispense with inflation. The power to command obedience enables it to achieve directly what formerly it could only achieve indirectly by inflation.

The consuming delusion is that because of what Americans were, this may not or cannot happen.

By a long lure of planned grass a society of bison may be decoyed to captivity in the Valley of Security.

In moments of uneasiness its bulls may be soothed by the voices of the herders saying: "You are free at any time to go back to the plains. Remember the grass there? It was poor and many of you were hungry."

There is no going back, because, first, these gentle

herders are rough with the few who try to start a stampede, and secondly, tame grass is sweet poison. From the eating of it the way of life on the plains is soon forgotten. To many whose stomachs were never so full before, even the memory of it is harrowing. If one asks, "But will the herders always be good to us?" another answers, "Nature was sometimes cruel."

RISE OF EMPIRE
1952

The Ancient Design
One

We have crossed the boundary that lies between Republic and Empire. If you ask when, the answer is that you cannot make a single stroke between day and night; the precise moment does not matter. There was no painted sign to say: "You now are entering Imperium." Yet it was a very old road and the voice of history was saying: "Whether you know it or not, the act of crossing may be irreversible." And now, not far ahead, is a sign that reads: "No U-turns."

If you say there were no frightening omens, that is true. The political foundations did not quake, the graves of the fathers did not fly open, the Constitution did not tear itself up. If you say people did not will it, that also is true. But if you say therefore it has not happened, then you have been so long bemused by words that your mind does not believe what the eye can see, even as in the jungle the terrified primitive, on meeting the lion, importuned magic by saying to himself, "He is not there."

That a republic may vanish is an elementary schoolbook fact.

The Roman Republic passed into the Roman Empire, and yet never could a Roman citizen have said, "That was yesterday." Nor is the historian, with all the advantages of perspective, able to place that momentous event at an exact point on the dial of time. The Republic had a long, unhappy twilight. It is agreed that the Empire began with Augustus Caesar. Several before him had played emperor and were destroyed. The first emperor in fact was Julius Caesar, who pretended not to want the crown, and once publicly declined it. Whether he feared more the displeasure of the Roman populace or the daggers of the republicans is unknown. In his dreams he may have seen a blood-stained toga. His murder soon afterward was a desperate act of the dying republican tradition.

His heir was Octavian, and it was a very bloody business, yet neither did Octavian call himself emperor. On the contrary, he was most careful to observe the old legal forms. He restored the Senate. Later he made believe to restore the Republic, and caused coins to be struck in commemoration of that event. Having acquired by universal consent, as he afterward wrote, "complete dominion over everything, both by land and sea," he made a long and artful speech to the Senate, and ended it by saying: "And now I give back the Republic into your keeping. The laws, the troops, the treasury, the provinces, are all restored to you. May you guard them worthily." The response of the Senate was to crown him with oak leaves, plant laurel trees at his gate and name him Augustus. After that he reigned for more than forty years and when he died the bones of the Republic were buried with him.

"The personality of a monarch," says Stobart, "had been thrust almost surreptitiously into the frame of a republican constitution.... The establishment of the Empire was such a delicate and equivocal act that it had been open to various interpretations ever since. Probably in the clever mind of Augustus it was intended to be equivocal from the first.[1]"

What Augustus Caesar did was to demonstrate a proposition found in Aristotle's *Politics*, one that he must have known by heart, namely this: "People do not easily change, but love their own ancient customs; and it is by small degrees only that one thing takes the place of another; so that the ancient laws will remain, while the power will be in the hands of those who have brought about a revolution in the state."

Revolution within the form.

Two

There is no comfort in history for those who put their faith in forms; who think there is safeguard in words inscribed on parchment, preserved in a glass case, reproduced in facsimile and hauled to and fro on a Freedom Train.

Let it be current history. How much does the younger half of this generation reflect upon the fact that in its own time a complete revolution has taken place in the relations between government and people? It may be doubted that one college student in a thousand could even state it clearly.

The first article of our inherited tradition, implicit in American thought from the beginning until a few years ago was this: *"Government is the responsibility of a self-governing people."*

That doctrine has been swept away; only the elders remember it. Now, in the name of democracy, it is accepted as a political fact that *people are the responsibility of government.*

The forms of republican government survive; the character of the state has changed. Formerly the people supported government and set limits to it and minded their own lives. Now they pay for unlimited government, whether they want it or not, and the government minds their lives—looking to how they are fed and clothed and housed; how they provide for their old age; how the national income, which is a product of their own labor, shall be divided among them; how they shall buy and sell; how long and how hard and under what conditions they shall work, and how equity shall be maintained between the buyers of food who dwell in the cities and the producers of food who live on the soil. For the last named purpose it resorts to a system of subsidies, penalties and compulsions, and assumes with medieval wisdom to fix the just price.

This is the Welfare State. It rose suddenly within the form. It is legal because the Supreme Court says it is. The Supreme Court once said no and then changed its mind and said yes, because meanwhile the President, who was the architect of the Welfare State, had appointed to the Supreme Court bench men who believed in it. The founders who wrote the Constitution could no more have imagined a Welfare State rising by sanction of its words than they could have imagined a monarchy; and yet the Constitution did not have to be changed. It had only to be reinterpreted in one clause—the clause that reads: "The Congress shall have power to lay and collect taxes, duties, imposts and excises, to pay the debts and provide for the common defense and general welfare of the United States."

"We are under a Constitution," said Chief Justice Hughes,[2] "but the Constitution is what the judges say it is."

The President names the members of the Supreme Court, with the advice and consent of the Senate. It follows that if the President and a majority of the Senate happen to want a Welfare State, or any other innovation, and if, happily for their design, death and old age create several vacancies on the bench so that they may pack the Court with like-minded men, the Constitution becomes, indeed, a rubberoid instrument.

The extent to which the original precepts and intentions of Constitutional, representative, *limited* government, in the republican form, have been eroded away by argument and dialectic is a separate subject, long and ominous, and belongs to a treatise on political science.

The one fact now to be emphasized is that when the process of erosion has gone on until there is no saying what the supreme law of the land is at a given time, then the Constitution begins to be flouted by executive will, with something like impunity. The instances may not be crucial at first and all the more dangerous for that reason. As one is condoned another follows and they become progressive.

To outsmart the Constitution and to circumvent its restraints became a popular exercise of the art of government in the Roosevelt regime. In defense of his attempt to pack the Supreme Court with social-minded judges after several of his New Deal laws had been declared unconstitutional, President Roosevelt wrote: "The reactionary members of the Court had apparently determined to remain on the bench for as long as life continued—for the sole purpose of blocking any program of reform."

Among the millions who at the time applauded that statement of contempt there were very few, if there was indeed one, who would not have been frightened by a revelation of the logical sequel. They believed, as everyone did, that there was one thing a President could never do. There was one sentence of the Constitution that could not fall, so long as the Republic lived.

The Constitution says: "The Congress shall have power to declare war." That, therefore, was the one thing no President could do. By his own will he could not declare war. Only Congress could declare war, and Congress could be trusted never to do it but by will of the people—or so they believed. No *man* could make it for them.

It is true that President Roosevelt got the country into World War II. That is not the same thing. For a declaration of war he went to Congress—after the Japanese had attacked Pearl Harbor. He wanted it, he had planned it, and yet the Constitution forbade him to declare war and he dared not do it.

Nine years later a much weaker President did.

After President Truman, alone and without either consent or knowledge of Congress, had declared war on the Korean aggressor, 7000 miles away, Congress condoned his usurpation of its exclusive Constitutional power. More than that, his political supporters in Congress argued that in the modern case that sentence in the Constitution conferring upon Congress the sole power to declare war was obsolete.

Mark you, the words had not been erased; they still existed in form. Only, they had become obsolete. And why obsolete? Because war may now begin suddenly, with bombs falling out of the sky, and we might perish while waiting for Congress to declare war.

The reasoning is puerile. The Korean war, which made the precedent, did not begin that way; secondly, Congress was in session at the time, so that the delay could not have been more than a few hours, provided Congress had been willing to declare war; and, thirdly, the President as Commander-in-Chief of the armed forces of the republic may in a legal manner act defensively before a declaration of war has been made. It is bound to be made if the nation has been attacked.

Mr. Truman's supporters argued that in the Korean instance his act was defensive and therefore within his powers as Commander-in-Chief. In that case, to make it Constitutional, he was legally obliged to ask Congress for a declaration of war afterward. This he never did. For a week Congress relied upon the papers for news of the country's entry into war; then the President called a few of its leaders to the White House and told them what he had done. A year later Congress was still debating whether or not the country was at war, in a legal, Constitutional sense.[3]

Three

A few months later Mr. Truman sent American troops to Europe to join an international army, and did it not only without a law, without even consulting Congress, but challenged the power of Congress to stop him. Congress made all of the necessary sounds of anger and then poulticed its dignity with a resolution saying it was all right for that one time, since anyhow it had been done, but that hereafter it would expect to be consulted.

At that time the Foreign Relations Committee of the Senate asked the State Department to set forth in writing what might be called the position of Executive Government. The State Department obligingly responded with a document entitled, "*Powers of the President to Send Troops Outside of the United States*—Prepared for the use of the joint committee made up of the Committee on Foreign Relations and the Committee on the Armed Forces of the Senate, February 28, 1951."

This document, in the year circa 2950, will be a precious find for any historian who may be trying then to trace the departing footsteps of the vanished American Republic. For the information of the United States Senate it said:

"As this discussion of the respective powers of the President and Congress has made clear, constitutional doctrine has been largely moulded by practical necessities. Use of the congressional power to declare war, for example, has fallen into abeyance because wars are no longer declared in advance.[4]"

Caesar might have said it to the Roman Senate. If constitutional doctrine is moulded by necessity, what is a written constitution for?

Thus an argument that seemed at first to rest upon puerile reasoning turned out to be deep and cunning. The immediate use of it was to defend the unconstitutional Korean precedent, namely, the declaration of war as an act of the President's own will. Yet it was not invented for that purpose alone. It stands as a forecast of executive intentions, a manifestation of the executive mind, a mortal challenge to the parliamentary principle.

The question is: "Whose hand shall control the instrument of war?"

It is late to ask. It may be too late, for when the hand of the Republic begins to relax another hand is already putting itself forth.

Properties of Empire
One

If you may have Empire with or without a constitution, even within the form of a republican constitution, and if also you may have Empire with or without an emperor, then how may the true marks of Empire be distinguished with certainty? What are they?

War and conquest? No. Republics may make war and pursue the aims of conquest. Continental conquest did not give the United States the character of Empire. Continental conquest was but the growth of a lively political organism, acting from its own center. The natural limits of it were geographic. Notions of Empire did at the same time arise—notions of external conquest—but they were sternly put down by the republican spirit.

Colonies, then? No, not colonies. At least, you have to say what you mean by colonies. They are of many kinds and represent diverse intentions in time and circumstance.

An over-populated republic may swarm, as bees do. Colonies did not make Greece an Empire. The Greek colonists were emigrants. As they moved across the Aegean Sea to the shores of Asia Minor they took with them fire from the sacred hearth, and were sometimes subsidized out of the public treasury as if they were children entitled to a farewell portion of the family wealth; but beyond that they were on their own, and when a colony was founded it was a sovereign state, not politically bound to the mother-state.

War, conquest, colonization, expansion – these are political exertions that occur in the history of any kind of state that was ever known, tyrannies, oligarchies, republics or democracies. But let us regard the things that belong *only* to empire, and set them down. Then we shall see.

Two

The first requisite of Empire is:

The executive power of the government shall be dominant.

It may be dominant originally, as in the days of hereditary kingship, or it may come to be dominant by change, as when the Roman republic passed under the rule of the Caesars.

As we now use the word *executive* it means much more than the Constitution intended. What the Constitution created was a government of three coequal powers, namely: (1) the Congress to make the laws, (2) a President to execute the laws, and (3) a Supreme Court to construe the laws, according to the Constitution. The Constitution was the supreme law, binding alike the Congress, the President and the Supreme Court itself. Each of these three powers could check the other two. This arrangement came to be called the American system of checks and balances.

The function of the Congress was legislative, the function of the President was executive and the function of the Supreme Court was judicial.

The President might veto a law enacted by the Congress, but by a two-thirds vote the Congress could pass it again over his veto and then it stood unless the Supreme Court said it was unconstitutional.

You will ask how that could work. If three coequal powers could annul one another's work, what would save the government from coming to an impasse?

What you are asking is, "Where in that triad was the sovereign power that could say the final word?" The answer is, "Nowhere." Then you may ask, "Is not sovereignty a vital attribute of national power?" It certainly is. Unless somewhere there is the sovereign power to say the final word, no government can long endure.

The founders gave more thought to that one problem than to all the others combined. They had to put sovereignty somewhere and they wished to make it safe, that is, safe beyond seizure. They thought it would not be safe in the hands of the President, nor in the hands of the Congress alone, and naturally it did not belong to the Supreme Court, for that was a judicial body. The solution was to put it in the hands of the people.

Only the people could say the last word. If they really wanted a law which the Supreme Court said was unconstitutional they could have it by changing the Constitution, and that they could do by a peaceable procedure set forth in the Constitution itself. For example, the Supreme Court said an income tax law that had been enacted by Congress and signed by the President was unconstitutional. But the people wanted that law. They amended the Constitution. Then the Congress enacted another income-tax law and the Supreme Court was obliged to say it was Constitutional. To amend the Constitution takes time; but that also was intended, the idea being to make the people reflect on what they are doing.

So it worked, and worked extremely well, for the Republic. It would not work for Empire, because what Empire needs above all in government is an executive power that can make immediate decisions, such as a decision in the middle of the night by the President to declare war on the aggressor in Korea, or, on the opposite side, a decision by the Politburo in the Kremlin, perhaps also in the middle of the night, to move a piece on the chess board of cold war.

For a century and a half the system of checks and balances worked like a self-correcting mechanism. Among the three coequal powers there was never a perfect balance; but any imbalance soon corrected itself. At one time there would be a very strong Supreme Court, as in the days of John Marshall; then again there would be a strong President and a weak Congress, or a strong Congress and a weak President.

The Federal income-tax law of 1914 gave the government unlimited access to wealth and, moreover, power for the first time to levy taxes not for revenue only but for social purposes, in case there should arise a popular demand for redistribution of the national wealth. World War I immediately followed. Looking backward we can see that these two events marked the beginning of a great rise in the executive power of government. It was slow at first, an imbalance such as had corrected itself before and might do so again. Indeed, during the 1920's it did seem to be correcting itself. Then came in rapid succession (1) the Great Depression, (2) the revolutionary Roosevelt regime, and (3) World War II, all within an arc of twenty years.

In those twenty years the sphere of Executive Government increased with a kind of explosive force.

Congress received from the White House laws that were marked "must." Its principal function was to enact and engross them. The part of the Supreme Court was to make everything square with the Constitution by a liberal reinterpretation of its language. The word *executive* came to have its new connotation. For all the years before when you spoke of the executive power of government you meant only the power to execute and administer the laws. Henceforth it would mean the *power to govern.*

A further, very subtle, change was taking place. Only a few years ago, if you had asked such a question as, "Who speaks for the people?" or "What organ of government utters their sovereign will?" the answer would have been "The Congress of the United States." Certainly. That was what the Congress was for.

Now it is the President, standing at the head of the Executive Government, who says: "I speak for the people," or "I have a mandate from the people." Thus the man who happens to be the embodiment of the executive principle stands between the Congress and the people and assumes the right to express their will.

There is more to this. Now, much more than Congress, the President acts directly upon the emotions and passions of the people to influence their thinking. As he controls Executive Government, so he controls the largest propaganda machine in the world, unless it be the Russian machine; and this machine is the exclusive possession of the Executive Government. The Congress has no propaganda apparatus at all and continually finds itself under pressure from the people who have been moved for or against something by the ideas and thought material broadcast in the land by the administrative bureaus in Washington. Besides the use they make of the Government Printing Office, these bureaus maintain 133 printing plants and 256 duplicating plants of their own. A further very subtle technique of propaganda is the intimate and confidential *briefing* of editors, writers, educators, and selected social groups on the government's point of view.

One of the task forces of the Hoover Commission looked at the government's propaganda machine and said:

"Every agency of government maintains its public relations staff.... Congress has been alert for several years to the organized pressure-group activities which are sponsored, supported and stimulated by the administrative agencies themselves. After fifteen months' work, Congressman Harness summarized his conclusions on government pressure-groups in these words: 'Everyone in Congress is keenly conscious of the tremendous power of this government propaganda machine, for he comes in direct contact with it every day.... Whether the immediate purpose of government propaganda is good or bad, the fact remains that individual liberty and free institutions cannot long survive when the vast powers of government may be marshaled against the people to perpetuate a given policy or a particular group of officeholders. Nor can freedom survive if all government policies and programs are sustained by an overwhelming government propaganda.'"

On "Our Most Dangerous Lobby," Representative Christian A. Herter[5] wrote: "Our Federal bureaucracy fought, bureau by bureau, every Congressional move to curb its innate urge to expand. Backed by its vast tax-supported propaganda machine and working through jobholders, also by well-meaning but misinformed citizens, it mustered almost overwhelming pressure for its continued growth. As weapons, it used distortion, misrepresentation and outright chicanery."

Senator Douglas[6] recently said there were three parties in Washington: a Democratic party, a Republican party and a Government party representing the departments, agencies and bureaus of Executive Government, and added that no pressure group was "more persistent and skilled in the technique of getting what it wants."

It was not only that as Executive Government proliferated the authority and prestige of Congress declined; a time came when Congress realized that a fourth entity called Government, with a solitary capital "G," was acting in a dimension of its own with a force, a freedom and a momentum beyond any control of the law-making power. Moreover, it was a thing so totally vast, so innumerable in its parts and so apparently shapeless that there was nowhere a mind able to comprehend it. That was when, in 1947, the Congress asked former President Hoover to organize a commission to study it scientifically and make it intelligible.

Such was the origin of the Commission on Organization of the Executive Branch of Government, Herbert Hoover chairman, now commonly referred to as the Hoover Commission. It created twenty-four task forces, each with a personnel suited to its special task, altogether three hundred men and women. They spent sixteen months exploring and charting the domain of Executive Government. Some of it was jungle, some of it was lawless, here and there were little bureaucratic monarchies that seemed to have grown up by themselves; and yet every part of it was very much alive and exercised powers of government, touching the lives of the people.

The full report of the Hoover Commission was never published; its bulk was too repellent. You may find it all in the archives. A summary of it—hardly more than a description of the bare bones of Executive Government together with anatomical suggestions for a better articulation of them—just that, made a book of more than 250 pages.

The Commission said:

"The executive branch is a chaos of bureaus and subdivisions. The gigantic and sudden growth of the executive branch has produced great confusion within the departments and agencies as well as in their relations to the President and to each other.

At the present time there are sixty-five departments, administrations, agencies, boards and commissions engaged in executive work, all of which report to the President—if they report to anyone. This number does not include the independent agencies in their quasi-judicial and quasi-legislative functions.

Some of these departments are larger than the whole government was twenty years ago."

The Commission found in the domain of the Executive Government more than thirty agencies engaged in lending money and public credit. (This number did not include Social Security and pension agencies.) In those more than thirty lending agencies the government had invested twelve and one-half billion dollars, and was obligated to invest nine billion more. Besides all that, the government was insuring more than eighty billion dollars of bank deposits, and had underwritten more than forty billion dollars of life insurance.

The Commission found that under the program called Grants-in-Aid the Federal government was paying two-fifths of the total cost of local government throughout the country and nearly one-sixth of the total cost of state government. "This," said the Commission, "has enlarged the executive branch, requiring great expansion in many departments and the establishment of new administrative agencies. It has increased national taxes. And it has been responsible to some extent for the rapid development of that fourth area of government known as the regional area, serviced in large part by Federal regional agencies."

Few realize in how many ways these activities of Executive Government touch our everyday business of living. Recently a writer at *Time Magazine* was doing an article on influence-peddling at Washington, and it occurred to him to drop into the middle of it the following paragraph:

"A big department store, for example, has to deal with some twenty Federal agencies (not to mention a score of state and municipal ones). The Bureau of Internal Revenue checks its taxes, the alcohol tax unit approves its whiskey labels, the Bureau of Customs stamps its imports, the Department of Labor's wages and hours division inspects its working conditions, the National Labor Relations Board hears its labor disputes, the Social Security Administration collects unemployment insurance, the Federal Reserve System administers credit regulations, the National Production Authority doles out scarce goods, the Securities and Exchange Commission patrols stock issues, the Federal Trade Commission scouts for mislabeling or deceptive advertising, the Post Office rules on parcel deliveries, the Selective Service Board makes passes at store executives and employees, the Interstate Commerce Commission rules on freight shipments, and if the store is hard up for capital the Reconstruction Finance Corporation has money to lend. In most of these departments, government agents have to make yes or no decisions on their own. The decisions often mean hundreds of thousands of dollars to the government, to a corporation or to an industry. If one has a few friends in the right places, who could ever draw the line between a legal and illegal favor?"

The Hoover Commission said: "Thousands of Federal programs cannot be directed personally by the President." Obviously not.

The result is Bureau Government, administered by bureaucrats who are not elected by the people.

In *The Grandeur that was Rome*, Stobart says that for a long time after the Republic had become an Empire a stout republican could still believe that he was governed by the Senate; yet little by little as a complete imperial bureaucracy was evolved the Senate sank into insignificance. It was really the bureaucracy of the imperial palace that governed the Roman world and strangled it with good intentions. The growth of the bureaucracy was both symptom and cause of the increasing power of the executive principle. The triumph of the system was the Edict of Prices, issued by Diocletian, fixing prices for every kind of commodity and wages for every kind of work.

The sad fact about the work of the Hoover Commission was that the necessity for Executive Government in all this new magnitude had to be assumed. That is to say, the Commission had no mandate to criticize the extensions of Executive Government in principle or to suggest that any of its activities might be discontinued. The limit of its assignment was to say how they might be organized for greater efficiency. *More efficient government; not less government.* An efficient bureaucracy, although it may cost less, is of course more dangerous to liberty than a bungling bureaucracy; and you may suppose that any bureaucracy, give it time and experience, will tend to become more efficient.

Aggrandizement of the executive principle of government takes place in several ways, mainly these:

(1) *By delegation.* That is when the Congress delegates one or more of its Constitutional powers to the President and authorizes him to exercise them. That procedure touched a very high point during the long Roosevelt regime, when an obliging Congress delegated to the

President, among other powers, the crucial one of all, namely, power over the public purse, which until then had belonged exclusively to the House of Representatives, where the Constitution put it.

(2) *By reinterpretation of the language of the Constitution.* That is done by a sympathetic Supreme Court.

(3) *By innovation.* That is when, in this changing world, the President does things that are not specifically forbidden by the Constitution because the founders never thought of them.

(4) *By the appearance in the sphere of Executive Government of what are called administrative agencies,* with the power to issue rules and regulations that have the force of law. This procedure also touched a high point during the Roosevelt regime. What it spells out is a direct delegation of legislative power by the Congress. These agencies have built up a large body of administrative law which people are obliged to obey. And not only do they make their own laws; they enforce their own laws, acting as prosecutor, jury and judge; and appeal from their decisions to the regular courts is difficult because the regular courts are obliged to take their findings of fact as final. Thus the Constitutional separation of the three governmental powers, namely, the legislative, the executive and the judicial, is entirely lost.

(5) *By usurpation.* That is when the President willfully confronts Congress with what in statecraft is called the *fait accompli*—a thing already done—which Congress cannot repudiate without exposing the American government to the ridicule of nations. It might be, for example, an executive agreement with foreign countries creating an international body to govern trade, in place of the International Trade Organization Treaty which the Senate would proba-

bly not have approved. This use of executive agreements, which take effect when the President signs them, in place of treaties, which require a two-thirds vote of the Senate, is a way of bypassing the Senate. It raises a number of fine legal questions which have never been settled.[7] The point is that the Constitution does not specifically forbid the President to enter into executive agreements with foreign nations; it provides only for treaties. In any case, when an executive agreement has been signed the Congress is very loath to humiliate the President before the world by repudiating his signature. Or again, it may be such a thing as going to war in Korea by agreement with the United Nations, without the consent of Congress, or sending troops to join an international army in Europe by agreements with the North Atlantic Treaty Organization.

(6) *Lastly, the powers of the Executive Government are bound to increase as the country becomes more and more involved in foreign affairs.* This is true because, both traditionally and by the terms of the Constitution, the province of foreign affairs is one that belongs in a very special sense to the President. There he acts with great freedom. It is only the President who can negotiate treaties. The limitations are two. The first one is that when he has signed a treaty it must be approved by a two-thirds vote of the Senate. This obstacle, as we have seen, may sometimes be avoided by signing to foreign countries executive agreements in place of treaties. The second limitation is that when the President appoints ambassadors to foreign countries they must be approved by the Senate; he may and does, nevertheless, send personal representatives on foreign errands. The restraining force of these two limitations is important only in the hands of a strong and hostile Congress. The controlling fact is that both the treaty-making power and the responsibility for conducting the coun-

try's foreign relations belong exclusively to the President; besides which, in both peace and war, he is Commander-in-Chief of the Armed Forces of the United States. The point of putting that in the Constitution was to make civil authority supreme over the military power.

So much for the rise in the executive power of government to a colossal dimension, in all our own time. It is no longer a coequal power; it is the dominant power in the land, as Empire requires.

Three

A second mark by which you may unmistakably distinguish Empire is: "*Domestic policy becomes subordinate to foreign policy.*"

That happened to Rome. It has happened to every Empire. The consequences of its having happened to the British Empire are tragically appearing. The fact now to be faced is that it has happened also to us.

It needs hardly to be argued that as we convert the nation into a garrison state to build the most terrible war machine that has ever been imagined on earth, every domestic policy is bound to be conditioned by our foreign policy.

The voice of government is saying that if our foreign policy fails we are ruined. It is all or nothing. Our survival as a free nation is at hazard.

That makes it simple, for in that case there is no domestic policy that may not have to be sacrificed to the necessities of foreign policy—even freedom. It is no longer a question of what we can afford to do; it is what we must do to survive. If the cost of defending not ourselves alone but the whole non-Russian world threatens to wreck our solvency, still we must go on. Why? Because we cannot stand alone. The first premise of our foreign policy is that without allies we are lost. At any cost therefore we must help them. If our standard of living falls, that cannot he helped.

We are no longer able to choose between peace and war. We have embraced perpetual war. We are no longer able to choose the time, the circumstance or the battlefield. Wherever and whenever the Russian aggressor attacks, in Europe, Asia, or Africa, there we must meet him. We are so committed by the Truman Doctrine, by examples of our intention, by the global posting of our armed forces, and by such formal engagements as the North Atlantic Treaty and the Pacific Pact.

Let it be a question of survival, and how relatively unimportant are domestic policies—touching, for example, the rights of private property, when, if necessary, all private property may be confiscated; or touching individual freedom, when, if necessary, all labor may be conscripted; or touching welfare and Social Security, when in a garrison state the hungry may have to be fed not by checks from the Treasury but in soup kitchens.

The American mind is already conditioned. For proof of that you may take the dumb resignation with which such forebodings as the following from the lead editorial of *The New York Times*, October 31, 1951, are received by the people:

"...the Korean war has brought a great and probably long-lasting change in our history and our way of life... forcing us to adopt measures which are changing the whole American scene and our relations with the rest of the world.... We have embarked on a partial mobilization for which about a hundred billion dollars have been already made available. We have been compelled to activate and expand our alliances at an ultimate cost of some twenty-five billion dollars, to press for rearmament of our former enemies and to scatter our own forces at military bases throughout the world. Finally, we have been forced not only to retain but to expand the draft and to press for a system of universal military training which will affect the lives of a whole generation. The productive effort and the tax burden resulting from these measures are changing the economic pattern of the land.

"What is not so clearly understood, here or abroad, is that these are no temporary measures for a temporary emergency but rather the beginning of a wholly new military status for the United States, which seems certain to be with us for a long time to come."

What a loss it would be to the Bible if the prophets had been editorial writers on *The New York Times*. Never before in our history, probably never before in any history, could so dire a forecast have been made in these level tones. But what they are saying is true. And certainly never before could people have felt so helpless about it, as if this were not the harvest of our foreign policy but Jehovah acting through the Russians to afflict us—and nobody else responsible.

Four

Another brand mark of Empire is: "*Ascendancy of the military mind, to such a point at last that the civilian mind is intimidated.*"

This we shall see.

The great symbol of the American military mind is the Pentagon in Washington with its seventeen and one-half miles of corridor, in which admirals and generals sometimes get lost; its twenty-eight thousand people at desks, eight thousand automobiles parked outside—the largest indoor city in the world. It was built at a cost of seventy million dollars during World War II, not as temporary housing such as was built during World War I, but as a dwelling for Mars. What it represents is a forethought of perpetual war.

There global strategy is conceived; there, nobody knows how, the estimates of what it will cost are arrived at; and surrounding it is our own iron curtain. The information that comes from the inner side is only such as the military authorities are willing to divulge, or have a reason for imparting to the people. All the rest is stamped "classified" or "restricted," in the name of national security, and Congress itself cannot get it. That is as it must be, of course. The most important secrets of Empire are military secrets. Even information that is without any intrinsic military value may be classified, on the ground that if it got out it might give rise to popular criticism of the military establishment and cause bad public relations.

If you want to know how and when it happened that this nation was legally converted into a garrison state for perpetual war, and with what anxiety the civilian mind made that surrender to the military mind, you may read the story in the *Congressional Record*, numbers 167, 168, and 170 (September 10, 11, and 13, 1951), where the closing debate takes place on "Department of Defense Appropriations, 1952."

The amount of money to be appropriated in that one bill was sixty-one billion dollars. But that was not all. Other appropriations would raise the total to roughly eighty-five billion.[8]

Everybody knew that here was more money than the Department of Defense could spend in a year. Moreover, it had on hand large unexpended balances from old appropriations. The Pentagon people said yes, that was true; they couldn't spend all that money in a year. But they wanted to have it on hand because they could make better long-term contracts if the suppliers knew for sure the cash would be there when the goods were delivered.

That was all of that.

Everybody knew the figures were miraculous. Billions could be invented on the Pentagon desks with pencil and scratch pad. It was so like doodling that a few billions could get lost when the papers were shuffled. One day when the Senate was struggling with a discrepancy in the printed figures—the difference between thirty-seven and forty-four billions—the Pentagon called on the telephone to say it had made an error of seven billion dollars.[9] Sorry. "And," said Senator Wherry[10], "we go on the theory that we know what we are talking about."

The Pentagon's revised figures were accepted.

All the secretaries and chiefs of staff had appeared before committees of Congress to say that their estimates had been reduced to the very granite of necessity. If Congress cut them the Department of Defense could not be held answerable for the nation's security. If the worst happened, the wrath of the people would be terrible. Let the Congress beware.

Senator Taft indulged the skeptical side of his nature. Only eighteen months before, in March, 1950 (that was three months before the beginning of the Korean War) the Chairman of the Joint Chiefs of Staff, General Bradley, had said to the Senate: "Yes, thirteen billion dollars a year is sufficient to provide for the security of the United States. If I recommend as much as thirty billion a year for the Armed Forces I ought to be dismissed as Chief of Staff." But now in one year they were asking for sixty-one billion. What had happened in the meantime? That was Mr. Taft's point. The Korean War had happened. But so far as the defense of the United States was concerned, nothing else had happened.

Senator Taft went on to say: "I do not know how long

this program is going to continue. My impression is that we shall have new weapons and new kinds of airplanes, and that we are embarked on expenditures of this kind for ten, fifteen, or twenty years, as one of the generals stated; and if that is so, I think it means an end of progress and the end of the freedom of the people of the United States.... We simply cannot keep the country in readiness to fight an all-out war unless we are willing to turn our country into a garrison state and abandon all the ideals of freedom upon which this nation has been erected. It is impossible to have such a thing in this world as absolute security.... I think we should appoint a commission to survey the military policy of the United States, to sit down with the military authorities and find out what we are trying to do, and to determine what is the proper scope of military activity in the United States."

Nevertheless, in the end he found himself unable to vote against the bill.

Everybody knew that a great deal of the money would be spent wastefully. The Senate had before it a report from the staff director of its own Committee on Expenditures in the Executive Departments, saying: "This is a frank admission that waste, extravagance and duplicate services presently exist in the Army, Navy, and Air Force."

To this the Pentagon people said: "You know very well that war is wasteful. Don't be stupid."

Senator Douglas rose. He dreaded what he was about to do. He dreaded it because he knew how quick the Department of Defense had always been to say that those who criticized its figures were trying to impair the military efficiency of the United States. That was the last thing he had in mind. He was for more preparedness, not less. "But," he continued, "unless we are to give up a representative democracy it is the function of Congress to scrutinize these expenditures. When we cease to scrutinize them, when we appropriate implicitly every dollar that is asked of us, then we shall have passed from being a representative democracy into being a militarized nation in which the General Staff makes the decisions."

He proposed to confine his scrutiny to the fringes. What he undertook to do, single-handed, was to squeeze out some of the bulging waste. He had served as an officer in the Marine Corps during World War II. He knew what he was talking about when he spoke of excess personnel, service plush and gravy trains. One by one his innocent amendments were resisted by Senator O'Mahoney[11], who was in charge of the bill, and who kept repeating the argument of the Department of Defense: "We cannot take every dollar of waste out of this bill. Waste is inherent in war and preparation for war."

Then at last, with the suavity of ice, Senator O'Mahoney rose to say that he should not like the galleries (where Russian correspondents might be listening), or the people, or the members of Congress, to understand the Senator from Illinois to be saying that our men in uniform were low in character, patriotism or devotion, because he was sure the Senator from Illinois did not mean to say that—not really.

(This from the record):

Mr. Douglas: Of course I did not mean that.

Mr. O'Mahoney: If the Senator will permit me—

Mr. Douglas: And neither do I wish—

Mr. O'Mahoney: The Senator will please permit me to continue.

With that, Senator Douglas was so overcome by a sense of hopeless frustration that he ran from the Senate chamber.

Three days later he voted for the bill, waste and all.

Senator Flanders[12] moved to send the bill back to Committee on Appropriations with instructions to cut six billion out of it. He was not thinking so much about saving the money; he was thinking that—"Unless we can set limits to the demands of the Defense Establishment it will continue to solidify its present control over our economy, over our standard of living and over our personal lives. There is no logical limit to the demands of a conscientious and patriotic Defense Establishment in times like these. No provision of arms and armament is enough. No expenditures are too great. This must be so in the nature of the case to those who by training and experience place their full faith in armed strength."

Senator O'Mahoney, speaking for the Committee on Appropriations, said: "Our committee will not know how to make these cuts. We shall have to call in the military again. We could not substitute our judgment for the judgment of the military men whom we have trained to do this job."

Senator Flanders' motion was defeated. He voted for the bill.

Senator Wherry said: "It is very difficult for any Senator to vote against a defense bill. But I believe the American people should know what we are getting into. This program and these appropriations will not stop this year or next year. The impact will be terrific and terrible upon the entire country."

He did not vote against the bill.

Senator Langer[13] moved to send the bill back to the Committee on Appropriations with instructions to put a fifty-six billion dollar ceiling on it.

Senator Dirksen supported the motion, saying: "There is a lot of guesswork in these figures. There is nothing sacred about a military figure. There is no staff, no expert accountant, nor anyone else, who is able to indicate firmly and precisely whether or not the estimates are reliable. Are we going to put the United States in a straightjacket?" Senator Langer's motion was voted down. Later both he and Senator Dirksen voted for the bill.

Senator Case[14] said: "There is one responsibility that rests upon every member of Congress, and that is to determine how much of the national income shall be taken in taxes or mortgaged and applied to any particular purpose. We have the responsibility of saying how much of the national income shall go to the national defense."

Senator O'Mahoney said: "Who am I to question the judgment of an admiral?"

When it came to a final vote the entire Senate said in effect: "Who are we to question the judgment of the military mind?"

Not a single vote was cast against the bill.

The intimidation of the civilian mind was complete and the Pentagon got its billions.

Only a few days before that, the Congress had passed a bill authorizing nearly six billion dollars for a military construction project—the largest bill of its kind ever passed in peace or war. One billion was for secret overseas bases within striking distance of Russia.

Of these secret bases Senator Russell,[15] of the Armed Services Committee, said: "These projects are highly classified. The committee inquired into them as best we could and concluded that in the light of the evidence submitted to us they were justified."

What a phrase from the Armed Services Committee of the United States Senate!—"as best we could." There obviously the civilian mind no longer governs.

Representative Richard B. Wigglesworth,[16] of the House Appropriations Committee, said: "Time and time again, no breakdown is available, fundamental information is not forthcoming from the military, and witnesses are unprepared to supply simple and essential facts."

Senator Francis Case said: "The moment anyone ventures a word of criticism or doubt about the amount of money any branch of the military services requests, the easy defense is to imply that he is in some way giving comfort and aid to the enemy."

In its report dated November 13, 1951, the Preparedness Subcommittee of the Senate Armed Services Committee, said: "One of the more alarming trends in military organization during the past few years has been the increasing administrative topheaviness of our Armed Forces." But it was General MacArthur himself who uttered these devastating words: "Talk of imminent threat to our national security through the application of external force is pure nonsense.... Indeed, it is a part of the general pattern of misguided policy that our country is now geared to an arms economy which was bred in an artificially induced psychosis of war hysteria and nurtured upon an incessant propaganda of fear. While such an economy may produce a sense of seeming prosperity for the moment, it rests on an illusionary foundation of complete unreliability and renders among our political leaders almost a greater fear of peace than is their fear of war."

The bald interpretation of General MacArthur's words is this. War becomes an instrument of domestic policy. Among the control mechanisms on the government's panel board now is a dial marked *War*. It may be set to increase or decrease the tempo of military expenditures, as the planners decide that what the economy needs is a little more inflation or a little less—but of course never any deflation. And whereas it was foreseen that when Executive Government is resolved to control the economy it will come to have a vested interest in the power of inflation, so now we may perceive that it will come also to have a kind of proprietary interest in the institution of perpetual war.

Yet in the very nature of Empire, the military mind must keep is secrets. A Republic may put its armor on and off. War is an interlude. When war comes it is a civilian business, conducted under the advice of military experts. Both in peace and war military experts are excluded from civilian decisions. But with Empire it is different; Empire must wear its armor. Its life is in the hands of the General Staff and war is supremely a military business, requiring of the civilian only acquiescence, exertion and loyalty.

Five

Another historic feature of Empire, and this a structural feature, is: *A system of satellite nations.*

We use that word only for nations that have been captured in the Russian orbit, with some inflection of contempt. We speak of our own satellites as allies and friends or as freedom-loving nations. Nevertheless, satellite is the right word. The meaning of it is *the hired guard*. When people say we have lost China or that if we lose Europe it will be a disaster, what do they mean? How could we lose China or Europe, since they never belonged to us? What they mean is that we have lost or may lose a following of dependent people who act as an outer guard.

From the point of view of Empire the one fact common to all satellites is that their security is deemed vital to the Empire; from the opposite point of view the common fact is that a satellite nation is one that is afraid to stand alone and wants the Empire's protection. So there is a bargain. The Empire, in its superior strength, assumes responsibility for the security and well-being of the satellite nation, and the satellite nation undertakes to stand with its back to the

Empire and face the common enemy. It may desert and go over to the enemy. That will be a change of position only, not a change of status. There will be one more satellite on the other side and one fewer on this side.

By this definition, our principal satellite is Great Britain. Since that relationship began, in 1940, the American government has contributed first to her defense and then to her postwar recovery gifts and loans equal to more than one-fourth her entire national wealth, and there is yet no end in sight. That would not have been for love. It could be justified to the American people only by the formula that the security of Great Britain is vital to the security of the United States. Nor is it sentiment that causes Great Britain to lean her weight against us, or to prefer, in the words of Lord Halifax,[17] "a relationship which cannot be dissolved," something like Mr. Churchill's proposed political wedlock. If she could stand alone she would. She would sooner have more satellites of her own than to be one.

And by the same definition, all the thirteen foreign countries that adhere to the North Atlantic Treaty are satellites. First of all, the Unites States assumes responsibility for their security. By the terms of the treaty, if any one of them is attacked, that shall be deemed an attack upon the United States itself. A fighting matter. Meanwhile, we give them billions for armaments, on the ground that if they will use the armaments to defend themselves they will at the same time be defending us. We do more than that. We underwrite their economic welfare and their solvency, on the theory that a wretched or insolvent satellite is not much good.

President Truman says: "We must make sure that our friends and allies overseas continue to get the help they need to make their full contribution to security and progress for the whole free world. This means not only military aid—though that is vital—it also means real programs of economic and technical assistance. It means helping our European allies to maintain decent living standards."

On the other side of the world, by the terms of the Pacific Pact, we assume responsibility for the security of Australia, New Zealand, and the Philippines; and by treaty we undertake to protect Japan from her enemies in return for military privileges.

It is a long list, and satellite traffic in the American orbit is already pretty dense without taking into account client nations, suppliant nations and waif satellites, all looking to the American government for arms and economic aid. These are scattered all over the body of the sick world like festers. For any one of them to involve us in war it is necessary only for the Executive Power at Washington to decide that its defense is somehow essential to the security of the United States. That is how the Korean war started. Korea was a waif satellite.

This vast system of entanglement, which makes a war anywhere in the world our war too, had its origin in the Lend-Lease Act, passed by Congress in March, 1941. That was in the second year of World War II and nine months before Pearl Harbor. The American people were resolved not to get into that war. Mr. Roosevelt persuaded them that the only way to stay out of it was to adopt "measures short of war." Churchill had promised: "Give us the tools and we will finish the job."

The Lend-Lease Act was entitled, "An Act to Promote the Defense of the United States." It was the single most reckless delegation of power by Congress to the President that had ever been made or imagined, amounting in fact to abdication. Literally, under the law, the President could have given away the United States Navy. When at a White House press conference that extreme point was made, the

President disposed of it derisively saying: "The law doesn't forbid the President of the United States to stand on his head, but he doesn't expect to stand on his head."

Under this law, the President was free, without limitation, without accountability to anyone, entirely by his own will—to give not only economic and military aid of any kind but secret military information also to any country "whose defense the President deems vital to the defense of the United States," and this "notwithstanding the provision of any other law." On the day the bill passed the President declared the defense of Great Britain vital to the defense of the United States; four days later he added China. When the war ended Lend-Lease goods were flowing to every non-enemy port in the world. The total cost was roughly fifty billion dollars. The principal beneficiaries were Great Britain, Russia, and France, in that order.[18]

Lend-Lease was for friends and allies during the war. After the war the American government distributed billions for the relief of human distress everywhere. Then came the Marshall Plan, which has already cost more than twelve billion dollars.

At first the Marshall Plan had no political meaning. The idea was that we were willing to share our wealth with Europe as a whole, to promote her postwar recovery. All European nations were invited to participate in that supernatural windfall, Russia included. But when Russia and her satellites spurned our capitalistic dollars, and then as the Russian mask began to slip, the character of the Marshall Plan changed. Its subsidies and benefits were for those countries of Western Europe that would align themselves against the Russian menace. The Marshall Plan was to have expired in 1951. It did not expire. Its name was changed. It is now the Mutual Security Plan. The Marshall Plan countries have become the North Atlantic Treaty countries, all looking to the American Empire for arms, economic aid and security.

"What we have tried to accomplish," said the Secretary of State[19] on returning from the first Brussels meeting of the North Atlantic Treaty Council—the British, French, Belgian, Dutch, and all the other North Atlantic Treaty nations—"what we have tried to accomplish has been in the light of a clear conception which we have all held. That is that the security of each one of us is tied up with the security of all of us, and therefore strength and security is a common problem and a common task. So far as the United States is concerned, that is a really national policy."

Mr. Acheson made that statement at a press conference on December 22, 1950. That was the beginning of the first officially organized evangel of fear to which the American mind was ever exposed.

A year later Senator Flanders was saying: "Fear is felt and spread by the Department of Defense in the Pentagon. In part, the spreading of it is purposeful. Faced with what seem to be enormous armed forces aimed against us, we can scarcely expect the Department of Defense to do other than keep the people in a state of fear so that they will be prepared without limit to furnish men and munitions.... Another center from which fear is spread throughout our people is the State Department. Our diplomacy has gone on the defensive. The real dependence of the State Department is in arms, armies and allies. There is no confidence left in anything except force. The fearfulness of the Pentagon and that of the State Department complement and reinforce each other."

Senator Flanders missed the point.

Empire must put its faith in arms.

Fear at last assumes the phase of a patriotic obsession. It is stronger than any political party. Any candidate for office who trifles with its basic convention will be scourged. The basic conviction is simple. We cannot stand alone. A capitalistic economy, though it possesses half the industrial power of the whole world, cannot defend its own hemisphere. It may be able to save the world; alone it cannot save itself. It must have allies. Fortunately, it is able to buy them, bribe them, arm them, feed and clothe them; it may cost us more than we can afford, yet we must have them or perish.

The voice of fear is the voice of government.

Thus the historic pattern completes itself. No Empire is secure in itself; its security is in the hands of its allies.

At the end of World War II General Marshall, then Chief of Staff, reported to the President, saying: "The security of the United States now is in its own hands." We had won the war and were coming home. Five years later, as Secretary of Defense, he was returning American troops and American armament to Europe as our contribution to an international army which, it might be hoped, would defend the security of the United States somewhere between the river Rhine and the Pyrenees.

Six

Fear may be understood. But a curious and characteristic emotional weakness of Empire is: *A complex of vaunting and fear.*

The vaunting is from what may be called that *Titanic* feeling. Many on the doomed *Titanic* would not believe that a ship so big and grand could sink. So long as it was above water her listing deck seemed safer than a lifeboat on the open sea. So with the people of Empire. They are mighty. They have performed prodigious works, even many that seemed beyond their powers. Reverses they have known but never defeat. That which has hitherto been immeasurable, how shall it be measured?

So those must have felt who lived out the grandeur that was Rome. So the British felt while they ruled the world. So now Americans feel.

As we assume unlimited political liabilities all over the world, as billions in multiples of ten are voted for the ever-expanding global intention, there is only scorn for the one who says: "We are not infinite. Let us calculate our utmost power of performance, weigh it against what we are proposing to do, and see if the scales will balance." The answer is: "We do not know what our utmost is. What we will to do, that we can do. Let us resolve to do what is necessary. Necessity will create the means."

Conversely, the fear. Fear of the barbarian. Fear of standing alone. Fear of world opinion, since we must have it on our side. The fear which is inseparable from the fact— that security is no longer in our own hands.

A time comes when the guard itself, that is, your system of satellites, is a source of fear. Satellites are often willful and the more you rely upon them the more willful and demanding they are. There is, therefore, the fear of offending them, as it might be only to disappoint their expectations.

Reflect on the subtle change that takes place in Anglo-American relations when we have our atomic bomb outpost in England, great bases there, a mighty air force in being, and thirty thousand military personnel. The Republic was not afraid to make the British lion roar when he was big and strong; now the State Department is uneasy if he ceases to make a purring sound. On Great Britain's part it is assumed that the United States cannot afford to let her down. On our part there is the beginning of awareness that if security is your treasure and you bury a part of it in the garden of a friend you have given hostage to friendship.

And then at last the secret, irreducible fear of allies—not this one or that one invidiously, but foreign allies in human principle, each with a life of its own to save. How will they behave when the test comes?—when they face, in this case, the terrible reality of becoming the European battlefield whereon the security of the United States shall be defended? If they falter or fail, what will become of the weapons with which we have supplied them? What if they are surrendered or captured and turned against us?

The possibility of having to face its own weapons on a foreign field is one of the nightmares of Empire.

Seven

As we have set them down so far, the things that signify Empire are these, namely:

(1) Rise of the executive principle of government to a position of dominant power,
(2) Accommodation of domestic policy to foreign policy,
(3) Ascendancy of the military mind,
(4) A system of satellite nations for a purpose called collective security, and,
(5) An emotional complex of vaunting and fear.

There is yet another sign that defines itself gradually. When it is clearly defined it may be already too late to do anything about it. That is to say, a time comes when Empire finds itself—

A prisoner of history.

The history of a Republic is its own history. Its past does not contain its future, like a seed.

A Republic may change its course, or reverse it, and that will be its own business. But the history of Empire is a world history and belongs to many people. A Republic is not obliged to act upon the world, either to change or instruct it. Empire, on the other hand, must put forth its power.

What is it that now obliges the American people to act upon the world?

As you ask that question the fear theme plays itself down and the one that takes its place is magnifical. It is not only our security we are thinking of—our security in a frame of collective security. Beyond that lies a greater thought.

It is our turn.

Our turn to do what?

Our turn to assume the responsibilities or moral leadership in the world.

Our turn to maintain a balance of power against the forces of evil everywhere—in Europe and Asia and Africa, in the Atlantic and in the Pacific, by air and by sea—evil in this case being the Russian barbarian.

Our turn to keep the peace of the world.

Our turn to save civilization.

Our turn to save mankind.

But this is the language of Empire.

The Roman Empire never doubted that it was the defender of civilization. Its good intentions were peace, law and order. The Spanish Empire added salvation. The British Empire added the noble myth of the white man's burden. We have added freedom and democracy. Yet the more that might be added to it the more it is the same language still. A language of power.

Always the banners of Empire proclaim that the ends in view sanctify the means. The ironies, sublime and pathetic, are two. The first one is that Empire believes what it says on its banner; the second is that the word for the ultimate end is invariably *Peace*. Peace by grace of force.

One must see that on the road to Empire there is soon a

point from which there is no turning back.

If it were true that our only hope of survival lay in collective security, then of course we should have to go on at any cost. If that were not true, still we should feel that we were obliged to go on for moral reasons. The argument for going on is well known. As Woodrow Wilson once asked, "Shall we break the heart of the world?" So now many are saying, "We cannot let the free world down." Moral leadership of the world is not a role you step into and out of as you like.

What does going on mean? You never know.

On June 24, 1941, as he extended Lend-Lease to Russia in World War II, President Roosevelt said:

"We will accept only a world consecrated to freedom of speech and expression—freedom of every person to worship God in his own way—freedom from want and freedom from terrorism."

Senator Taft was one of the very few at that time who could imagine what going on from there might mean. He asked: "Will that part of the world which Stalin conquers with our airplanes and our tanks be consecrated to freedom of speech and expression? Will it be consecrated to freedom from want and freedom from terrorism? Or, after a Russian victory with our aid, must we step in with our armies to impose the four freedoms on two hundred million people, ten thousand miles away, who have never known freedom from want or freedom from terrorism?" In October, 1951, only ten years later, *Collier's* magazine devoted one entire issue to a preview of World War III, with twenty articles written by professors, military people, publicists and others who might call themselves makers of public opinion—and the sequel of it was *the liberation of the Russian people.* The answer to Mr. Taft's question.

As the Eighty-second Congress blindly voted the

Pentagon its billions, the specter of a garrison state was the principal witness. Moving like a mist through the entire debate was the premonition that these steps were irreversible. Nobody could imagine how expenditures of such magnitude could continue for an intermediate time. Nobody could seriously hope they were going to be less the next year, or the year after that, or for that matter ever. For suppose the great war machine were finished in five years. What could we do but to begin and build it all over again, with more and more terrible weapons, at greater and greater cost? Nobody could hope that the demands of our allies and friends were going to be less. Yet no one could imagine how to stop. No one could even suggest a way to go back.

Eight

Now the voice of persuasion, saying: "Let it be Empire. It will be Empire in a new sign. For the first time in the history of mankind it happens that the paramount power of the world is in the keeping of a nation that has neither the will to exploit others nor any motive to increase its wealth at their expense. It wants only to chain the aggressor down, and then a world in which all people shall be politically free to govern themselves and economically free to produce and exchange wealth with one another on equal terms.

"Are Americans afraid of their own power? Shall they forbear to use it to bring their vision to pass lest it react upon them adversely or do their traditions an injury? What of the traditions? We did not inherit them to begin with. We created them. Now, shall our strength be bound by swaddling clothes? Or shall we have the courage to come of age in a new world?"

The view may be sublime. That will not save you if, as you reach for the stars, you step in a chasm.

It is true that Empire may be a great civilizing force. The Roman Empire was. The Augustan Age was not equaled again for a very long time—not again until the Victorian Age of the nineteenth century, and that was the British Empire.

But it is true also that this *is* Empire in a new sign and there lies the chasm.

Every Empire in history that endured at all, even those that did greatly advance civilization, somehow made it pay. And why not? Is there any good without price?

Rome exported peace, law, and order; but not for nothing. Her imports were food, wine, luxuries, treasure and slaves. She laid her satellites under tribute, and when the cost of policing the Roman world and defending the Roman peace was more than her satellites were willing to pay, the Empire fell.

There was a price for *Pax Britannica*. The British Empire did not lay direct tribute upon her satellites. There was a better way. She so managed the terms of trade that the exchange of manufactured goods for food and raw materials was very profitable for England; and as year after year she invested her profits in banks and ports and railroads all over the world she grew very rich and her navy ruled the seas. Again, why not? Could a few million people in the British Isles, when it came their turn, afford to police the world for nothing ? When the terms of trade began to turn against them—that is, when the people who exchanged food and raw materials for the high-priced products of British machines began to revolt, the Empire was in trouble. Yet, while it lasted it was the most civilizing force the world had known since the Roman Empire.

Never in any world, real or unreal, has it been imagined before that Empire, out of its own pocket, should not only pay all the costs of Empire, but actually pay other nations for the privilege of giving them protection and security, defending their borders and minding their economic welfare. That indeed is Empire in a new sign. The chasm is bankruptcy.

Not to make sense of it, which is impossible, but only in order not to forget that you belong to a race of once rational creatures, you have to keep telling yourself that it all began when you walked through the looking glass.

That we pay Europe to let us defend European civilization; that we give steel to Europe because the European production of steel is limited for political reasons; that we give coal to Europeans when the one thing they have plenty of is coal, and do this only to save them from the alternative of either mining enough of their own coal or freezing; that we increase our own national debt to give Great Britain the money to reduce her national debt, on the ground that that will be good for her credit; that when, from buying more American goods than she can pay for, over and above what we give her, Europe goes from one financial crisis to another, called the crisis of the dollar gap, we put more billions in her pocket to enable her to go on buying more than she can pay for (that is what the Marshall Plan was for)—well, even though all of this could be comprehended in the formula that the security and comfort of our friends and allies may be essential to the defense of American liberty, the Mad Hatter is still to be heard from.

The formula is not confined to Europe. It acts with a kind of centrifugal force, to scatter dollars all over the world.

Thus, we find ourselves defending the American way of life by engaging in such projects as the following:

In the colonial territories of Great Britain: Road development in Nyasaland, Nigeria, Sierra Leone, the Gold Coast, Northern Rhodesia, North Borneo, Sarawak, and

Malaya; reservoir construction in Somaliland, an agricultural equipment pool in Mauritius, locust control in the Middle East and East Africa, a lumber project in British Borneo, drainage and irrigation in British Guiana, a Gold Coast railroad, and so forth.

In the colonial territories of France: Road development in French West Africa, the French Cameroons, and French Equatorial Africa; water and power distribution and workers' housing in Casablanca, steam power plants at Bone and Oran in Algeria, agricultural services and wheat storage in Algeria, water supply in the Brazzaville area of French Equatorial Africa, irrigation and stock watering in the Masso Valley of Morocco, a rayon pulp plant, and so forth.

In the Belgian Congo: Soil survey, waterways, roads and a power project.

At Portuguese Angola: A meat industry project.

In Burma: Irrigation, flood control, soil conservation, control of livestock diseases, agricultural extension work, canning, rice storage, cotton seed improvement, harbor development, low-cost housing, public health activities, education, technical assistance, audiovisual service, and so forth.

In Indo-China: Road development, Cambodia fisheries, irrigation, river transportation, water purification, firefighting equipment, public health, low-cost housing, a radio school, information service, and so forth.

In the Indonesian Republic: Fisheries, a forest project, control of foot-and-mouth disease, rehabilitation of the textile industry, improvement of native industries, public health services, and so forth.

In Thailand: Irrigation, agricultural research and development, deep freezing, harbor development, roads, a railroad shop, mineral development, planned communications, technical assistance, and so forth.

Enough of that. A complete list would be too long. These, you understand, are but the fringe activities. They represent only spillings from the great Marshall Plan pool, after it had provided dollars for industrial projects in Austria, Belgium, Denmark, France, Germany, Greece, Iceland, Italy, the Netherlands, Norway, Portugal, the United Kingdom, and Turkey.

Casting out only those areas around which the Russians have drawn their hard red line, if there is a country or a land in the whole world where the American government's planners, experts and welfare-bringers are not passing miracles with dollars, it is because the State Department's map maker either forgot it or couldn't spell it and thought it might never be missed.

This is Imperialism of the Good Intent.

It is Empire as Franklin Delano Roosevelt imagined it when he said, of Lend-Lease: "What I am trying to do is to eliminate the dollar sign." During the next ten years one hundred billion dollars' worth of American wealth was cast upon the waters, as gifts, grants, subsidies and unrepayable loans to foreign countries. And none of it has ever come back.

Empire of the Bottomless Purse.

The Lost Terrain
One

Between government in the republican meaning, that is, *Constitutional, representative, limited* government, on the one hand, and Empire on the other hand, there is mortal enmity. Either one must forbid the other or one will destroy the other. That we know. Yet never has the choice been put to a vote of the people.

The country has been committed to the course of Empire by Executive Government, one step at a time, with slogans, concealments, equivocations, a propaganda of fear, and in every crisis an appeal for unity, lest we present to the world the aspect of a divided nation, until at last it may be proclaimed that events have made the decision and it is irrevocable. Thus, now to alter the course is impossible. If that were true, then a piece of writing like this would be an exercise in pessimistic vanity.

Who says it is impossible? The President says it; the State Department says it; all globalists and one-worlders are saying it.

Do not ask whether or not it is possible. Ask yourself this: If it were possible, what would it take? How could the people restore the Republic if they would? or, before that, how could they recover their Constitutional sovereign right to choose for themselves?

When you have put it that way you are bound to turn and look at the lost terrain. What are the positions, forgotten or surrendered, that would have to be recaptured?

Two

The height in the foreground is a state of mind. To recover the habit of decision the people must learn again to think for themselves; and this would require a kind of self-awakening, as from a wee small alarm in the depths. This is so because thinking has been laid under a spell. The hypnotic powers are entrenched, combative and dangerous. But once the self-liberated mind had regained that first height it would see not only that there *is* an alternative course but that above the noxious emanations of fear and the fog of propaganda the view of it is fairly clear.

On December 20, 1950, Herbert Hoover pointed to it, saying "The foundation of our national policies must be to preserve for the world this Western Hemisphere Gibraltar of Western Civilization. We can without any measure of doubt, with our own air and naval forces hold the Atlantic and Pacific oceans, with one frontier on Britain (if she wishes to co-operate); the other on Japan, Formosa, and the Philippines. We could, after initial outlays for more air and navy equipment, greatly reduce our expenditures, balance our budget and free ourselves from the dangers of inflation and economic degeneration.

"We are not blind to the need to preserve Western Civilization on the continent of Europe or to our cultural and religious ties to it. But the prime obligation of Western Continental Europe rests upon the nations of Europe. The test is whether they have the spiritual force, the will and acceptance of unity among them by their own volition. America cannot create their spiritual forces; we cannot buy them with money."

His words were lost on the spellbound American mind. The government's propaganda smothered him. He was an isolationist back from the grave.

Will you take a military authority for it, even though it speaks against itself? Addressing the American Legion at Miami on October 17, 1951, General MacArthur said:

"It is impossible to disassociate ourselves from the affairs of Europe and Asia. Major warfare in either has become our immediate military concern, lest they fall under the domination of those hostile to us and intent upon predatory incursions against our own land."

The global thesis, as any globalist would state it. Then amazingly in the same speech, three paragraphs later, MacArthur said:

"There are many of the leaders and people of Western Europe who mistakenly believe that we assist them solely to protect ourselves, or to assure an alliance with them, should our country be attacked. This is indeed fallacious thinking. Our potential in human and material resource, in alignment with the rest of the Americas, is adequate to defend this hemisphere against any threat from any power or any association of powers."

The fascinated American mind hardly noticed this startling discrepancy in MacArthur's reasoning. If the American hemisphere is invulnerable, then why do we have to defend American liberty in Europe, Asia, and Africa? The question is not arguable here. The purpose of asking it is merely to show that it does exist.

In *A Foreign Policy for Americans*[20], Senator Taft evidently thought he was discussing the principles of foreign policy, whereas in fact he was discussing only its history and its faults and how now to go on with it, saying: "I see no choice now except to rely on our armed forces and alliances with those nations willing to fight the advance of communism."

Then he adds one sentence, as honestly he must, saying: "In my opinion we are completely able to defend the United States itself."

There the discrepancy again. If we are completely able to defend the United States itself, why do we have to rely upon allies?

The Pentagon itself has plotted an alternative course. That fact is not disclosed by the government, on the ground that to disclose it would be, in its opinion, contrary to the public interest. Military support for the government's course, that may be disclosed, that is in the public interest. If it be denied that the Pentagon has an alternative plan, the answer is that in such a case the people ought to fire the General Staff and get a new one. If it is still permitted for people to say what they will defend and how they will defend it—to choose, for example, whether to save the United States or save the whole world—why should they not have all the military information there is? Why should the government withhold part of it? Whose property is it? Does it belong to the government or to the people? Strategy must be secret. We do not speak of strategy. We speak of national policy.

Three

The second height to be regained is that where of old foreign policy was submitted to public debate. How long ago that seems! And how was that height lost? There was no battle for it. The government seized it without a struggle; and now the President may say the people ought to accept the government's foreign policy without debate.

In a speech to the National Women's Democratic Club on November 20, 1951, President Truman said: "You remember what happened in 1920. When the people voted for Harding, that meant a tremendous change in the course of the United States was following. It meant that we turned our backs on the new-born League of Nations…. I think most people now recognize that the country chose the wrong course in 1920…. Since I have been President I have sought to steer a straight course of handling foreign policy matters on the sole basis of the national interest. The people I have chosen to fill the major positions concerned with foreign policy have been picked solely on merit, without regard to party labels. I want to keep it that way. I want to keep our foreign policy out of domestic politics."

So far had the American mind been conditioned by the infatuate phrase, *bipartisan foreign policy*, that this extraordinary statement was vacantly received. What was the President saying? He was saying that because, in his opinion, the people once voted wrong on foreign policy, they ought not to vote on it at all any more. Let them leave it to the President. It follows logically that the people have no longer anything to say about war and peace.

On this height, where foreign policy once more shall be debated by the people who may have to die for it, let the wind be cold and merciless. Let those be nakedly exposed to it who have brought the country to this impasse, who so misunderstood the nature of what they have done that they find no ignominy in having brought national security to rest upon the good will of boughten allies—if it is so; who petted and nourished the Russian aggressor and recommended him to the affections of the American people as a peace-loving collaborator. If they can justify themselves to the free and disenthralled intelligence of the people, so that the people knowingly choose to go on with them, then there will be nothing more to say, or to do, but decently to perform the obsequies of the Republic. Until this is settled it will be useless to discuss domestic policies because what is at stake in the first case is the fate of the republican form of government.

Four

On the next height lies control of the public purse. Until the people have recovered that, they cannot tame Executive Government. Passing laws to control or restrain it is of no avail whatever. The only way to reason with it is to cut it off at the pockets. Until the Roosevelt Revolution, even from colonial days until then, no popular prerogative was so jealously guarded as this one. The colonists insisted on paying the royal governors out of colonial funds, because if they were paid by the British Treasury they would be too independent. And when it came to setting up the American government, the Constitution said that control of the purse should be in the hands of the House of Representatives because that was the popular side of Congress. The people have not always managed the purse well. They have sometimes stuffed it with bad money; they have sometimes flung its contents around in a reckless manner. But there is this difference, that no matter how badly the people may manage the public purse it cannot control them, whereas in the hands of the government the control of the purse becomes the single most powerful instrument of executive policy touching the lives of the people.

Five

There is no valley to cross to the next height. It is right there. On top of it is the nesting place of the Fallacious Serpent. The spirit of insatiable evil inhabits the serpent; the evil is inflation. Its weapon of defense is an invisible vapor, the effect of which is to cause the people to become economic alcoholics, afflicted with the delusion that they can get rich by destroying the value of money. It is no good to think of cutting off its head. It has millions of heads, all in the likeness of human heads, and as fast as they are chopped off others appear in place of them. Moreover, at this point, even in the ranks of the dragon hunters, dissensions will break forth, people saying: "Don't kill him. If he dies deflation will come, and deflation is worse. Only chain him down." At that every one of the heads begins to grin in a most sardonic manner. The serpent thinks its life is safe and to wiggle out of chains is its morning exercise. There is only one thing to do with the monster. It can be sickened and starved, not to death, because the life in it is immortal, but to a harmless shadow. Its food is irredeemable paper money. Sound money is its poison. Victory here cannot be unconditional. You will have to leave a guard, and then someone to watch the guard, and then keep going back to see.

Six

The positions in the lost terrain that have been named are vital. To serve the Republic they must all be stormed and captured. Others are important, but if these are taken the others can wait; but there is still one more, the last and highest of all, and as you approach it you may understand the serpent's sardonic grin. The slopes are steep and barren. No enemy is visible. The enemy is in yourself. For this may be named the Peak of Fortitude.

What you have to face is that the cost of saving the Republic may be extremely high. It could be relatively as high as the cost of setting it up in the first place, one hundred and seventy-five years ago, when love of political liberty was a mighty passion, and the people were willing to die for it.

When the economy has for a long time been moving by jet propulsion, the higher the faster, on the fuel of perpetual war and planned inflation, a time comes when you have to choose whether to go on and on and dissolve in the stratosphere, or decelerate. But deceleration will cause a terrific shock. Who will say, "Now!" Who is willing to face the grim and dangerous realities of deflation and depression?

When Moses had brought his people near the Promised Land he sent out scouts to explore it. They returned with rapturous words for its beauties and its fruits, whereupon the people were shrill with joy, until the scouts said: "The only thing is, this land is inhabited by very fierce men."

Moses said: "Come. Let us fall upon them and take the land. It is ours from the Lord."

At that the people turned bitterly on Moses, and said: "What a prophet you have turned out to be! So the land is ours if we can take it? We needed no prophet to tell us that."

No doubt the people know they can have their Republic back if they want it enough to fight for it and to pay the price. The only point is that no leader has yet appeared with the courage to make them choose.

ENDNOTES

Notes to THE REVOLUTION WAS

1. *Politics*, Book IV, Part V. The modern translation by Benjamin Jowett is less dramatic: "For governments do not change at once; at first the dominant party are content with encroaching a little upon their opponents. The laws which existed previously continue in force, but the authors of the revolution have the power in their hands."

2. De Lawd (the Lord) is a character in *The Green Pastures*, a 1929 play by Marc Connelly based on Roark Bradford's story, "Ol' Man Adam an' His Chillun." In the play, Southern blacks act out stories from the Old Testament. The play won a Pulitzer Prize in 1930 and was made into a movie in 1936 starring Richard B. Harrison as De Lawd.

3. Roosevelt spoke of the New Deal's changes, which then included the wage and price controls of the Blue Eagle, becoming "a permanent feature of our modernized industrial structure." Then he said, "It is to the eternal credit of the American people that this tremendous readjustment of our national life is being accomplished peacefully, without serious dislocation, with only a minimum of injustice, and with a great, willing, spirit of cooperation throughout the country."

4. Attributed to Oliver Wendell Holmes Sr., 1809-1894, poet and father of Supreme Court Justice Oliver Wendell Holmes Jr.

5. The brothers Tiberius (163-133 B.C.) and Gaius (158-122 B.C.) Gracchus each briefly led Rome toward using state policy to aid the poor. One measure was for the state to buy wheat and sell a fixed amount to each citizen at about half the market price.

6. Jacob Burckhardt, 1818-1897, a Swiss liberal and philosopher of history, wrote: "What we are wont to regard as moral progress is the domestication of individuality brought about a) by the versatility and wealth of culture and b) by the vast increase in power of the state over the individual..." *Reflections on History* (U.K., 1943), p.62.

7. Robert A. Taft, 1889-1953, son of President Howard Taft, was elected senator from Ohio in the anti-Roosevelt tide of 1938 and served until his death. Torch-bearer for the Republican conservatives, he opposed economic controls under the New Deal and FDR's efforts to get into World War II before Pearl Harbor. He stuck with an America-first policy after the war, opposing the draft, NATO and Truman's undeclared war in Korea. Taft tried for the Republican nominations in 1940, 1948 and 1952, but was edged out by more liberal candidates—Wilkie, Dewey and Eisenhower, respectively.

8. Carter Glass, 1858-1946, senator from Virginia 1920-1946, was the pre-

New-Deal Democrats' voice on currency. He wrote the Federal Reserve Act of 1913, which created a central bank to issue gold-backed money, and had written the provision of the Democratic platform of 1932 that read, "We advocate a sound currency to be preserved at all hazards." On April 27, 1933, he rose in the Senate to protest. "Why are we going off the gold standard?" he said. "With nearly 40% of the entire gold supply of the world, why are we going off the gold standard?... To me the suggestion that we may devalue the dollar 50% means national repudiation. To me it means dishonor. In my conception of it, it is immoral."

9. Frank C. Walker, 1886-1959, was a founding member of the Roosevelt for President Society in 1931. He followed FDR from New York to Washington, becoming Postmaster General 1940-1945. When Roosevelt decided to dump his left-wing vice president, Henry Wallace, for Harry Truman, he chose Walker to break the news to Sen. James Byrnes, who had wanted on the ticket.

10. When he closed the banks and forbade transfers of money out of the country, Roosevelt cited as legal authority the Trading With the Enemy Act. This had been passed in 1917 to allow President Wilson to embargo Imperial Germany. The law applied only during war, but on March 9, 1933, Congress modified it to apply during "any other period of national emergency declared by the President," thereby approving what Roosevelt had done. The Trading With the Enemy Act was used recently against Americans who traveled to Saddam Hussein's Iraq to donate medicine in defiance of the embargo.

11. Ownership of gold certificates remained illegal until April 24, 1964, and gold bullion, until Dec. 31, 1974. Gold clauses in private contracts remained illegal until Oct. 27, 1977.

12. The HOLC, 1933-1935, provided mortgages with public money. It was replaced by the Federal Housing Administration (FHA) in 1934, which used government guarantees to marshal private money, and by the Federal National Mortgage Association (Fannie Mae) in 1937, which bought the FHA-guaranteed mortgages. FHA and Fannie Mae still exist.

13. This was the equivalent of $46 billion in 2003 dollars, or 71 percent of the entire federal budget for the fiscal 1933 year, then ending.

14. *U.S. v. Bankers Trust Co.* 294 U.S. 240 (Gold clauses in private contracts); *Nortz v. U.S.* 294 U.S. 317 (Gold backing for paper money); *Perry v. U.S.* 294 U.S. 330 (Gold backing for Treasury bonds), all decided 5-4 for the government.

15. Attributed to a speech by Lenin in 1923 to the Commissars of Education.

ENDNOTES

16. Subtitled *A Chicago Study*, this 1939 book by Harold D. Lasswell and Dorothy Blumenstock was a content analysis of the writings of the Communist Party, U.S.A. It was reprinted in 1970 by the Greenwood Press.

17. A reference to *Whose Constitution? An Inquiry into the General Welfare* (1936), by Henry Wallace, the New Deal Secretary of Agriculture who ordered the plowing up of cotton and the kiling of little pigs. From 1941 to 1944 Wallace was vice president, after which he was dumped by Democratic kingmakers for being too left-wing. In 1948 he ran for president as the candidate of the pro-Soviet Progressive Party.

18. A reference to Roosevelt's statement to the press on May 31, 1935, after the Supreme Court struck down the National Recovery Administration, that "we have been relegated to the horse-and-buggy definition of interstate commerce."

19. Another sample of what is now called "class warfare" rhetoric is from Roosevelt's State of the Union address for 1936:
    "We have earned the hatred of entrenched greed. The very nature of the problem that we faced made it necessary to drive some people from power and strictly to regulate others. I made that plain when I took the oath of office in March, 1933. I spoke of the practices of the unscrupulous money-changers who stood indicted in the court of public opinion. I spoke of the rulers of the exchanges of mankind's goods, who failed through their own stubbornness and their own incompetence. I said that they had admitted their failure and had abdicated.
    "Abdicated? Yes, in 1933, but now with the passing of danger they forget their damaging admissions and withdraw their abdication. They seek the restoration of their selfish power ... autocracy toward labor, toward stockholders, toward consumers, toward public sentiment. Autocrats in smaller things, they seek autocracy in bigger things ...
    "The challenge faced by this Congress is more menacing than merely a return to the past—bad as that would be. Our resplendent economic autocracy does not want to return to that individualism of which they prate, even though the advantages under that system went to the ruthless and the strong. They realize that in thirty-four months we have built up new instruments of public power. In the hands of a people's Government this power is wholesome and proper. But in the hands of political puppets of an economic autocracy such power would provide shacles for the liberties of the people. Give them their way and they will take the course of every autocracy of the past—power for themselves, enslavement for the public."

20. Seventy years later, subsidies are pouring out at the rate of about $18 billion a year. Since 1930 the percentage of Americans working on the farm has fallen from 30% to 2%, and still there are too many in farming.

21. The percentage of workers belonging to unions jumped sharply in the 1930's, peaked in the 1950's at about 35 percent and has fallen since. By 2003 in the private sector it had fallen to 8.2%, about what it was before the New Deal. The law of which Garrett complains, the National Labor Relations Act, continues to give unions the privilege of organizing workers in groups by majority vote rather than by individual sign-up. But America's experience of unionism, its need to compete and its economic ideas, have weakened the support for unions.

22. The director of budget Garrett refers to was no doubt Lewis Douglas, 1894-1974. An heir to the Phelps Dodge copper fortune (Douglas, Ariz., is named for his father) and a Democratic congressman 1927-1933, Douglas was FDR's first budget director. He quit in mid-1934 in protest to the New Deal. He went on to a career in government and business, including a stint as ambassador to Britain, 1947-1950, and director of General Motors, 1944-1965.

     In his Godkin Lectures at Harvard in May 1935, Douglas argued that the doctrine of a planned economy "verges upon an authoritarian, tyrannical State." His lectures were published as *The Liberal Tradition* (1935)—apparently in counterpoint to "The Progressive Tradition," an article in the April 1935 *Atlantic Monthly* by the New Deal's guru of central planning, Rexford G. Tugwell. The story Garrett relates here is not in Douglas's book, but the anlysis in the book is similar to Garrett's:

     "In the light of a deliberate spending policy, which, if not stopped, must certainly destroy our currency ... in the light of references by Administration officials to the 'New Economic Order', to the 'Third Economy'--in the light of [quoting Tugwell] 'We shall need no firing squads, no guillotines, no deportations or concentration camps' --in the light of a policy of complete regimentation and an evidenced inclination to prosecute it, it is not strange that there are some who entertain suspicions with respect to the ultimate design." (pp 88-89)

23. Traitors, after Vidkun Quisling, 1887-1945, the traitor who invited Hitler to occupy Norway. The Germans did, and made Quisling a "puppet" premier from 1942 to 1945. At war's end the restored government of Norway had him executed.

24. Gen. Hugh Johnson, 1882-1942, was draft administrator during World War I and served as Army liason to the War Industries Board, which directed war production. From 1933 until 1935 he headed the National Recovery Administration (NRA), the New Deal agency inspired by the War Industries Board. The NRA set maximum hours and minimum wages, and replaced market prices with industry-negotiated codes. Every business was urged to display its symbol, a blue eagle clenching a gear wheel and lightning bolts, and there were public parades to promote it. It was Roosevelt's most radical program, and was struck down by the Supreme Court in the "sick chicken" case, *A.L.A. Schechter Poultry Corp. v. U.S.*, 295 U.S. 285 (1935).

ENDNOTES

25. Several that exist in 2004 under the same names are the Social Security Board (SSB), the Federal Deposit Insurance Corp. (FDIC), the Securities and Exchange Commission (SEC) and the National Labor Relations Board (NLRB). The Fair Labor Standards Act of 1938 (FLSA) is still law, and the Department of Labor still has a Wage Hour Division (WHD) that enforces its rule of time-and-a-half wages for overtime work of employees that it deems "non-exempt".

26. The House Un-American Activities Committee (HUAC) existed from 1938 to 1969. It was, and is, an ogre figure for the Left because of its hearings in 1947 on communist influence in Hollywood. They (the Left) argue that government should not concern itself with ideology in films, and that innocents were hurt. Perhaps so; but it should also be admitted that there *were* a lot of communists in Hollywood and they did affect the content of films. (See Kenneth Lloyd Billingsley's *Hollywood Party: How Communism seduced the American Film Industry in the 1930's and the 1940's* (1998)). HUAC also was the venue for outing communist spies, including Alger Hiss, whose identity as a spy was confirmed in the 1990s by Soviet files that were made public.

27. In March 1937 the United Auto Workers, which had just won recognition from General Motors, ralllied an estimated 15,000 to Cadillac Square. This was during Roosevelt's campaign against the Supreme Court, and while the Court was considering a case that challenged the pro-union law, the National Labor Relations Act. A few days later, in "the switch in time that saved Nine", the court ruled in favor of the NLRA and the minimum wage, ending its fight against the New Deal.

28. The Tennesssee Valley Authority was formed in 1933 to build dams and market public power in parts of seven states. In his message to Congress asking for the TVA law, April 10, 1933, Roosevelt said, "If we are successful here we can march on, step by step, in a like development of other great natural territorial units within our borders."

   They never quite did it the TVA way, which combines the poweres of government and private enterprise. In the *Saturday Evening Post* of May 7 and 28, 1938, Garrett wrote of TVA's directors, appointed by the president: "Never before had the Congress delegated so much power to three men or to any board. It was the power to set up a regional government within the United States; one that nobody elected, one that could not be changed or voted away by the people on whom it acted."

   Two-thirds of a century later, the TVA could be described with the same words. It is the largest producer of power in the United States and the largest emitter of nitrous oxide, because most of its power is from coal. It has some $30 billion in debt, and, despite huge tax advantages over its private-utility neighbors, it has power rates higher than many of of theirs.

29. This was the Supreme Court case of *Wickard v. Filburn*, 317 U.S. 111

(1942). This established the principle that even small acts, neither interstate nor commercial, might be federally regulated as interstate commerce if many people doing them might *affect* interstate commerce (in this case, by lowering the demand for wheat). *Wickard* is still part of American law.

30. Probably referring to Alf Landon, governor of Kansas 1933-37 and the Republican candidate for president in 1936. Garrett had campaigned for him and knew him.

31. The Reconstruction Finance Corp. was established in 1932 under President Hoover. The RFC lent money to cash-strapped banks and railroads. It was expanded under Roosevelt and reached its height during World War II, when it financed war plants and foreign aid. It was shut down in 1956 after a scandal over favoritism.

32. This was over the Guffey Coal Act, which restored price controls over coal producers similar to the NRA's, which had just been declared unconstitutional. As Roosevelt feared, the Court found the Guffey Coal Act unconstitutional as well. The case was *Carter v. Carter Coal Co.* 298 U.S. 238 (1936).

33. From Lincoln's "House Divided" speech to the Illinois Republican convention, June 17, 1858, in which he famously said, "I believe this government cannot endure permanently half-slave and half-free."

Notes to EX AMERICA

1. The loan referenced was actually a $3.7 billion ($37 billion in 2003 dollars) 50-year loan at 2%, made in 1946. It was controversial in America because Britain had just voted in a Labour government that was beginning to nationalize industry, and people said American taxpayers were financing British socialism.

2. The treaty, signed February 6, 1922, limited capital ships to a ratio of U.S. and U.K. 5, Japan 3, France and Italy 1.67. It expired in 1936 when Japan insisted on parity with the U.S. and the U.K.; they refused and Japan withdrew.

3. The first bracket of the 1914 income tax was 1% of taxable income greater than $20,000, which exempted 98% of earners from paying any tax at all. The top bracket was 7% of income greater than $500,000. Income tax was not withheld from paychecks until World War II.

4. The actual line from Wilson's speech to the Senate, July 10, 1919, after he returned from Europe with the League of Nations treaty was, "Dare we reject it and break the heart of the world?" Writes Thomas Fleming, "This

was the only memorable line of his speech. But not a single newspaper picked it up and converted it into a slogan, as they had with 'the war to end wars' or 'making the world safe for democracy' ... The speech was a flop." *The Illusion of Victory* (2003) p. 393. On March 19, 1920, the Senate voted 49-35 for the treaty, seven votes short of the two-thirds required for approval.

5. Albert W. Hawkes, 1878-1971, a Republican, served one term in the Senate, 1943-1949, representing Garrett's home state.

6. Harry Elmer Barnes, 1889-1968, sociologist and revisionist historian, was acclaimed in the 1920s and 1930s as a brilliant progressive. When he came out against Roosevelt's interventionism in the late 1930s he was no longer welcome in establishment circles. A symposium edited by Barnes, *Perpetual War for Perpetual Peace: A Critical Examination of the Foreign Policy of Franklin Delano Roosevelt*, was published by Caxton Press in 1953. In it Barnes called for "the traditional American foreign policy of benign neutrality."

7. Unbeknownst to Henry Stimson, Nov. 25 was the day the Japanese government gave the go-ahead for the attack on Pearl Harbor. Stimson, 1867-1950, had been Taft's secretary of war and Hoover's secretary of state, and had been brought into FDR's government in 1940 as a pro-war Republican. He supported the internment of the West Coast Japanese Americans and the use of the atomic bomb on Hiroshima and Nagasaki, although he insisted the bomb not be dropped on the historic city of Kyoto.

8. To Garrett, the clock started March 11, 1941, when Congress approved Lend-Lease military aid. The first naval combat, which is what Adm. Stark referred to, was Sept. 4, between a U-boat and the U.S. destroyer *Greer*, which had been patrolling near Iceland. Roosevelt claimed, in a radio address Sept. 11, that the U-boat had fired first and that it was part of "a Nazi design to abolish freedom of the seas." He ordered U.S. forces in the Atlantic to shoot Axis warships on sight. On Oct. 14, Stark reported that the *Greer* had tracked the sub for hours and radioed its location to British planes, which bombed it. Senator Burton K. Wheeler, Dem. -Mont., cited a letter from a crewman saying the *Greer* had fired first.

    The *Greer* had not been hit. On Oct. 17, the U.S. destroyer *Kearny* was hit but not sunk by U-boat torpedoes, killing 11 crewmen. On Oct. 31, the U.S. destroyer *Reuben James* was sunk, killing 100 Americans—all before Pearl Harbor.

9. Arthur Watkins, 1886-1973, Republican of Utah, was senator from 1947 to 1959. He was known as an expert on Indian affairs and for being chairman of the committee that recommended censure of Sen. Joseph McCarthy.

10. The book *Holism and Evolution* (1926) by Jan Christiaan Smuts argues that

evolution is a progression toward ever more complicated integrations. Smuts, 1870-1950, led Boer guerrillas against the British, made his peace with them and led South African troops against German East Africa in World War I. He was prime minister in World War II, when South Africa was again a British ally. In 1948 he lost office to the Nationalists, who proclaimed the policy of apartheid.

11 Everett Dirksen, 1896-1969, Republican of Illinois, served in the House 1933-1949 and the Senate 1951-1969, the last eleven years as minority leader. He was a compromiser well regarded by Democrats and is known for rounding up Republican votes for the Civil Rights Act of 1964.

12. Cordell Hull, 1871-1955, Democrat of Tennessee, served in the House for all but two of the years 1907-1931, and helped write the income tax law of 1913 and the inheritance tax law of 1916. An internationalist and free trader, Hull served as Roosevelt's secretary of state 1933-1944. Hull received the Nobel Peace Prize in 1945, but was often overshadowed in foreign affairs by FDR and others favored by the president.

13. *The Economic Consequences of the Peace* (1919), Chapter 6. The full quote is noteworthy:

> Lenin is said to have declared that the best way to destroy the capitalist system was to debauch the currency. By a continuing process of inflation, governments can confiscate, secretly and unobserved, an important part of the wealth of their citizens. By this method they not only confiscate, but they confiscate arbitrarily; and, while the process impoverishes many, it actually enriches some. The sight of this arbitrary rearrangement of riches strikes not only at security, but at confidence in the equity of the existing distribution of wealth. Those to whom the system brings windfalls, beyond their deserts and even beyond their expectations or desires, become 'profiteers,' who are the object of the hatred of the bourgeoisie, whom the inflationism has impoverished, not less than of the proletariat. As the inflation proceeds and the real value of the currency fluctuates wildly from month to month, all permanent relations between debtors and creditors, which form the ultimate foundation of capitalism, become so utterly disordered as to be almost meaningless; and the process of wealth-getting degenerates into a gamble and a lottery.
>
> "Lenin was certainly right. There is no subtler, no surer means of overturning the existing basis of society than to debauch the currency. The process engages all the hidden forces of economic law on the side of destruction, and does it in a manner which not one man in a million is able to diagnose."

14. Henry Morgenthau Jr. 1891-1967, was Roosevelt's secretary of the treasury 1934-1945. He had been a friend of FDR, who as governor of New York, in 1929 had appointed him chairman of the New York State Agricultural

Advisory Commission. Morgenthau went on to borrow more for the government than all the previous treasury secretaries combined.

15. Social Security met the problem of inflation by indexing benefits, increasing the tax rate from 2% to 12.4% and by raising the tax base. The problem today is the drop in the birth rate that began four years after Garrett died, and increases in longevity. The ratio of workers to retirees was 16-1 in 1950; it is 3.3-1 in 2004 and is projected to be 2-1 in 2042. By present calculations, Social Security goes cash-negative in 2018, is propped up by money from general taxes (via the "trust fund") and collapses in 2042.

16. It wasn't a crash; the American economy has had milder recessions with paper money than it had with gold money. The price has been inflation: the paper dollar of 2003 was worth 7 cents in the gold dollar of 1933, and its value falls every year. The appetite of the federal government, which was about 5% of gross domestic product at the beginning of the New Deal and 9.8% in 1940, has been about 20% in the half-century since Garrett's death.

Notes to RISE OF EMPIRE

1. John C. Stobart, *The Grandeur That Was Rome: A Survey of Roman Culture and Civilization*, 1912. A classic reference reprinted in many editions up to 1971.

2. Chief Justice Charles Evans Hughes, 1862-1948, a Republican, was named to the Supreme Court by President Taft, quit to run for the presidency in 1916, lost, and was named to the Court again by President Hoover. He administered the oath of office to Roosevelt, but ruled against him in most of the early New Deal cases. In 1937 he defected to FDR's side in "the switch in time that saved Nine." Jettisoning the doctrine of freedom of contract in the minimum-wage case, *West Coast Hotel v. Parrish* 300 U.S. 379 (1937) he wrote, "What is this freedom? The Constitution does not speak of freedom of contract."

3. No declaration of war has been voted since 1941. Recent practice has been for presidents to ask Congress for permission to conduct larger wars, while denying that permission is necessary. They do it because the people demand it.

For the Vietnam war, the Tonkin Gulf Resolution of August 1964 was approved 416-0 in the House and 88-2 in the Senate, the near-unanimous vote reflecting the belief that a destroyer had been attacked twice without provocation. In 1973, in the backwash of the Vietnam war, Congress passed the War Powers Resolution, which prohibits the president from a major foreign deployment lasting more than ninety days. President Nixon said it was unconstitutional and vetoed it. Congress overrode his veto. Presidents have since followed the War Powers Resolution while asserting that it is unconstitutional.

The Gulf war resolution of January 1991 passed 250-183 in the House and 52-47 in the Senate. The Kosovo war resolution of March 1999, authorizing air attacks only, passed 58-41 in the Senate but failed 213-213 in the House, which then defeated one resolution to declare war, another to pull out, passed a resolution to forbid the use of ground troops and another vaguely supporting "military operations." The Iraq war resolution of October 2002 passed 296-133 in the House and 77-23 in the Senate, though President Bush claimed that he could have started the war based on the resolution of 1991.

4. Congressional Record, March 20, 1951, p.2745.

5. Christian Herter, 1899-1966, Republican of Massachusetts, was a Representative 1943-1952. An internationalist, he helped pass the Marshall Plan over the objection of conservatives led by Robert Taft. Herter was Eisenhower's last secretary of state, 1959-1961, replacing John Foster Dulles.

6. Paul Douglas, 1892-1976, a professor of economics, a Unitarian and a supporter of Socialist Norman Thomas in 1932, came to embrace the New Deal and Roosevelt's policy of challenging the Axis. He served as a Democratic senator from Illinois 1949-1967, and supported unions, welfare and civil rights.

7. The body created in 1947 in place of the proposed International Trade organization was the General Agreement on Tariffs and Trade (GATT), which, in the 1990s, became the World Trade Organization. The WTO agreement amounts to a treaty, but it is called a "congressional-executive agreement." That way, approval required simple majorities of the Senate and House rather than two-thirds of the Senate, which it would not have got. The idea of the congressional-executive agreement came out of the Roosevelt administration. Its legality has still not been settled by the Supreme Court, but is assumed to have been validated by time.

8. In 2003 dollars, which are worth less than 15 cents in those dollars, about $570 billion.

9. In 2003 dollars, an error of about $47 billion.

10. Kenneth Wherry, 1892-1951, Republican of Nebraska, a lawyer, was elected to the Senate in 1942, and was Republican whip 1947-1949 and minority leader 1949-1951.

11. Joseph O'Mahoney, 1884-1962, Democrat of Wyoming, lawyer, senator 1933-1961.

ENDNOTES

12. Ralph Flanders, 1880-1970, Republican of Vermont, inventor in the machine-tool industry, senator 1946-1959.

13. William Langer, 1886-1959, Republican of North Dakota, lawyer, senator 1941-1959.

14. Francis Case, 1896-1962, Republican of South Dakota, newspaper editor and publisher, senator 1951-1962.

15. Richard Russell, 1897-1971, Democrat of Georgia, lawyer, governor of Georgia 1931-1933, senator 1933-1971.

16. Richard Wigglesworth, 1891-1960, Republican of Massachusetts, was a U.S. official in Berlin in the mid-1920s involved with German debts and war reparations. He served in the House of Representatives 1928-1958.

17. Named Edward Wood, 1881-1959, the man who became Lord Halifax was born with an atrophied arm with no hand, but to a lord and lady with a castle. He served in the House of Commons and as viceroy of India before being named war secretary under Conservative Prime Minister Stanley Baldwin in 1936. Halifax had several dealings with Hitler, including the Munich Pact, and was pegged as an appeaser. By the time Churchill came to power in May 1940, Halifax's backbone had stiffened. Churchill kept him on as war minister until December 1940, then named him ambassador to the United States, a position he kept to may 1945.

18. In 2003 dollars, it totaled about $520 billion, 60% to Britain, 20% to the Soviet Union, and 20% to France, China and others.

19. Dean Acheson, 1893-1971, was educated at Harvard Law School and became private secretary to Supreme Court Justice Louis Brandeis and, in 1933, undersecretary of the Treasury. Acheson was Harry Truman's secretary of state, 1945-1953, dealing with the Marshall Plan, NATO and the containment of Russia. He was blamed by conservatives for tolerating communists in the State Department and for tolerating pro-communist foreign service officers who undermined the Chinese government of Chiang Kai-shek.

20. Doubleday, 1951.

Index

INDEX

159

Other thought-provoking
titles from
CAXTON PRESS:

ANTHEM
by Ayn Rand
ISBN 0-87004-124-x
Hardcover $12.95

WHAT SOCIAL CLASSES OWE EACH OTHER
by William Graham Sumner
ISBN 0-87004-165-5
Paperback $6.95

THE ART OF CONTRARY THINKING
by Humphrey B. Neill
ISBN 0-87004-110-x
$17.95

SALVOS AGAINST THE NEW DEAL
by Garet Garrett
ISBN 0-87004-425-7
$12.95

DEFEND AMERICA FIRST
by Garet Garrett
ISBN 0-87004-433-8
$13.95